DWIGHT MARGRAVE'S
1940-1946
JOURNEY

THE LETTERS

WORLD WAR II

IN GOD WE TRUST

FORWARD

My first reading of our Grandfather's letters was in 2012 after my Mother spent the better part of a year sorting, organizing, and transcribing them into several Word documents. Upon her completion she had them photocopied and spiral bound at the local copy store to easily share with the family. When I received the completed bound copy of what my Mom referred to as, "her Dad's letters," I set it aside and said, "thanks Mom, I'll read it when I get some free time." Several weeks passed with the binder sitting on my end table, I casually picked it up one evening and started to read. I could not put it down until I finished the last letter.

The story told in these letters is about a young man who served his country as a support person in the military rather than on the battlefield. These raw and authentic glimpses of my Grandfather's unique experience is something not only captivating to me, but is sure to serve as an intriguing insight for the millions of other Americans whose family members served in World War II.

The journey that unfolds with each letter demonstrates hallmarks of the human condition that still hold true today—struggles with loneliness, boredom, learning a new job, getting along with people, and navigating life with the uncertainty of the future; but also the joys accompanied with self-discovery, entertainment, a change of scenery, and above all else, love and family. These letters also remind us how much our society has changed in just a few generations –from the prices of food and commodities to the physical hardships a young man in need of work or in military service endured during this time period. Remarkably, the descriptions of these hardships are written in a matter-of-fact tone with reassurances to the reader that he is "doing ok" despite extraordinary circumstances.

As I read each letter, I felt a genuine and unexpected connection to the experiences my Grandfather Dwight was writing home about. I also felt great sense of pride and gratitude for my mother who took the time and energy to share these letters with her family. I hope that others who read this artfully curated book of letters also feel connected to both the humanistic and historical value of these writings.

STEFANIE JOHNSON MONAHAN

granddaughter

TRANSCRIBED
Julia Margrave Steere

DESIGNED
Christofer Johnson

RESEARCH
Richard Steere

FORWARD
Stefanie Monahan

SCANNING
Skyler Johnson

COPY EDITING
Dennis Molina & David Kinigson

INDEPENDENTLY PUBLISHED BY LUICE DESIGN, INC., LAKE WORTH FL 33460
FIRST PRINTING 2020, U.S.A.

www.LettersHomeTheBook.com

ISBN: 9798564421416
Imprint: Independently published

Copyright 2020 by Luice Design, Inc. All rights reserved. No portion of this book may be reproduced, mechanically, electronically or by any other means without written permission of the publisher.

T/3 Dwight Earl Margrave 1946.

"Sorry Dad, but these letters are too important to keep for ourselves. Our country needs to be reminded of the bravery your generation had, to keep our country, and build it."

—Julia Margrave Steere

> Sipan
> July 1 - 45
>
> Dear Folks:
> I was very disappointed with you when I heard that you had one of my letters published in the paper. Please don't ever do that again, because I am not in this d— army for any publicity — and on top of that you will have me in the doghouse with my wife. Oh well I guess there is nothing to do but forget it.
>
> Don't have much to write about, as the censor is very strict. Has been pretty hot here but always cool at nite, the food is still good

Letter from Dwight to his parents from Sipan - 1945.

AS EVER, *Dwight*

Earl Margrave, Jack Grant, Pearl Margrave, Dwight Margrave, Alta Grant, Ehel, Gene Brom, Fay Hill - 1918.

ACKNOWLEDGEMENTS

First and foremost I am eternally grateful to my Grandmother Pearl Margrave for saving all of Dwight's letters and then passing them down to my Aunt Marjorie Keyser, Dwight's sister. She kept them for over 30 years before handing them off to me for preservation.

I am forever grateful to my son, Christofer Johnson who invisioned the letters in a new light and brought them to life with his graphic design talents for many generations to read.

I would like to thank my beloved husband Richard Steere for all of his encouragement, input and editing... but most of all his patience during this emotional project.

I want to thank my daughter Stefanie Monahan for her dedicated help in edits and encouragement. I also thank Zachary Monahan, William Margrave, Skyler Johnson, David Keyser, and Dennis Molina for their valuable input and contributions to the making of this book.

And last but not least I am so grateful to my father for his service to this nation and his family.

Julia Margrave Steere

OCEAN RIDGE, FLORIDA U.S.A.

2020

AS EVER, *Dwight*

*American fighter fly in formation over the USS MISSOURI during surrender ceremonies.
Tokyo Bay, Japan. Sept. 2, 1945. World War II.*

DEDICATED TO ALL THE GENERATIONS WRITING HOME

1900 - 1924
THE G.I. GENERATION

1925 - 1945
SILENT GENERATION

1946 - 1964
BABY BOOMERS

1965 - 1979
GENERATION X

1980 - 2000
MILLENNIAL

2001 - NOW
ZOOMER

Howe, Neil. Generations: The History of America's Future, 1584 to 2069.

AS EVER, *Dwight*

SPRING LAKE

DWIGHT EARL MARGRAVE
A SOLDIER'S JOURNEY THROUGH WWII

RANCH

Spring Lake Ranch, Sandhills of Nebraska, USA - 1930's.

AS EVER, *Dwight*

DWIGHT EARL MARGRAVE
Gordon High School Class of 1934
Gordon, Nebraska U.S.A.

INTRODUCTION

64 years after the end of World War II, my father's sister gave me a bundle of old letters held together by a rubber band. My father had written these letters before, during, and immediately after the end of World War II to his parents, he called them his folks .

I remember once asking my Father about World War II and he told me it was unspeakable. That was the end of that conversation.

History is never silenced, hidden away perhaps, but brought forth when it serves a purpose to enlighten us all.

Dwight Earl Margrave was one of America's Greatest Generation: Extraordinary, brave, selfless, and patriotic generation.

Dwight was born on June 13, 1916 to his parents, Earl Irwin Margrave and Pearl Ireland Margrave. His birth place was Sheridan County, Nebraska. His Indian father and his white mother were ranchers in the great Sandhills of Nebraska. They ranched for nearly 40 years on the Spring Lake Ranch.

My Father's Father, Earl Margrave, was a member of the Sac and Fox Indian Tribe of northeastern Kansas. The Sac and Fox Nation of Missouri in Kansas and Nebraska is one of three federally recognized Native American tribes of Sac and Meskwaki (Fox) peoples. Their name for themselves is Nemahahaki and they are an Algonquian people and Eastern Woodland culture. I mention this because during my research on the Army Ordinance Division, in which Dwight served, there is a Sac and Fox connection.

Title to a 900 acre island was acquired through a treaty with the chiefs of the Sac and Fox Indian Tribes in November 1804. It is situated well to the south of the main channel of the Mississippi River between Illinois and Iowa. In 1835 the island became the site of a western armory that became to be known as the Rock Island Arsenal. Pioneer settlements in the Illinois territory lead the government to establish a frontier post on the extreme northwestern point of the island that was named Fort Armstrong.

Dwight Margrave's Childhood at
Spring Lake Ranch, Nebraska U.S.A.
Circa 1920

AS EVER, *Dwight*

NUMBER		INDIAN NAME	ENGLISH NAME		RELATIONSHIP	DATE OF BIRTH	SEX
Last	Present						
*36	34	Ash-kah-pah-kah-pa-se	Koshiway, David	15	Bro.	1887	M
*37	35	Tuas-que-to	" Jonathan	14	"	1883	M
38	36		Lasley, Walter	95	Bro.	1895	M
39	37		" Pearl	97	Sis	1899	F
*40	38		" John	96	Bro.	1898	M
*41	39		LeClair, Julia	58	Mother	1868	F
42	40		" Walter	99	son	1900	M
*43	41		" William	59	"	1889	M
*44	42		LeClair, Margaret	98		1896	F
*45	43		Margrave, James T.	63	Father	1880	M
*46	44		" Margaret	100	dau.	1905	F
47	45		" William H.		son	1906	M
48	46		" James Stuart		son	1912	M
*49	47		Margrave, Earl	64	Father	1883	M
50	48		" Dwight Earl		son	1916	M
*51	49	(Willie C. Margrave)	Margrave, William C.	65	Father	1876	M
52	50		" Julia	102	dau.	1903	F
*53	51		" H. J.	101	son	1900	M

Year: 1922; Roll: M595_394; Page: 3; Line: 15; Agency: Pottawatomie
Indian Census Rolls, 1885-1940; (National Archives Microfilm Publication M595, 692 rolls);
Records of the Bureau of Indian Affairs, Record Group 75; National Archives, Washington, D.C.

Like his Father, Dwight always had one foot in the white man's world and one foot in the Indian world.

He graduated from high school in 1934, during the Great Depression. In 1938, (like his father) he joined the Mason's. He was like many young men of that time who went west and north seeking their fortunes, or just to make enough money to send back home to their families. Dwight had experienced enough of the tough life of cattle, horses, cowboys, and Indians.

Like many young men in Dwight's generation, he wrote in the first person. I have taken the liberty to use the personal "I" in transcribing his letters. This edification is for clarity.

Fort Richardson, AK

Camp Shilo, Manitoba, CAN

Seattle, WA

Gordon, NE
Fort Crook, NE

New York City, NY

San Francisco
Harbor, CA

Camp Perry, OH   Aberdeen, MD
Washington D.C.

Tennessee Maneuvers, TN   Ft. Bragg, NC
Ft. Leavenworth, KS   Ft. Fisher, NC
Camp Rucker, AL
Camp Shelby, MS

DWIGHT'S JOURNEY

began in 1940, Gordon, Nebraska, taking him throughout North America and sailing to the Pacific Theater. He returned home in 1946.

AS EVER, *Dwight*

TABLE OF

1940 - Dwight leaving for Seattle posing with his mother Pearl Margrave.

1940	PAGE 26
1941	PAGE 42
1942	PAGE 90
1943	PAGE 142

CONTENTS

1940 - Dwight leaving for Seattle posing with his father Earl Margrave.

1944	**PAGE 170**
1945	**PAGE 252**
1946	**PAGE 340**
POST WAR	PAGE 352

DWIGHT EARL MARGRAVE
A SOLDIER'S JOURNEY THROUGH WWII

1940
LET THE JOURNEY BEGIN

Dwight on "Pop Eye" summer of 1936 Gordon, Nebraska.

AS EVER, *Dwight*

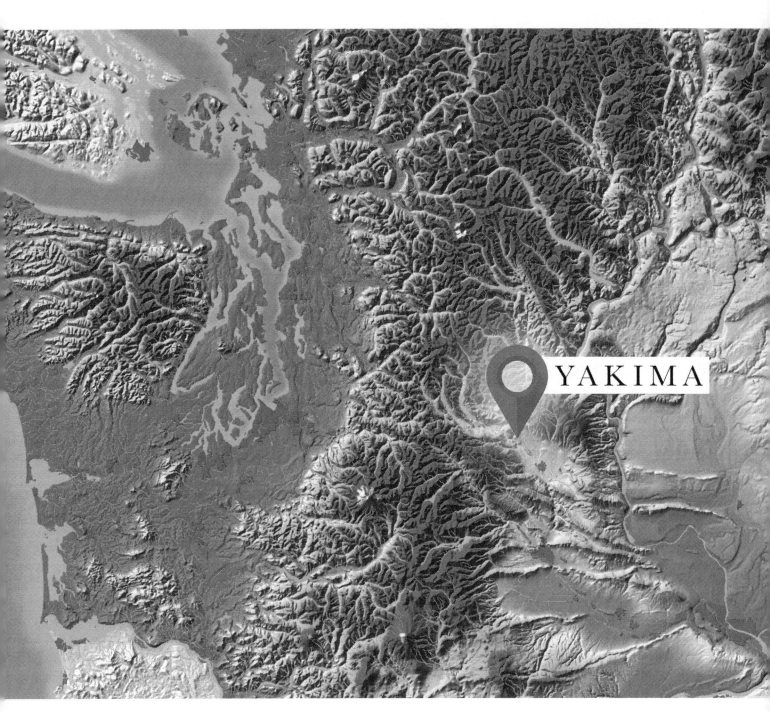

Topography map of Washington State.

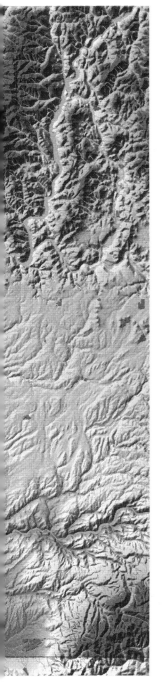

YAKIMA WASHINGTON

Circa 1940

Yakima is the county seat of Yakima County, Washington. Yakima is located 60 miles southeast of Mount Rainier. It is in the Yakima Valley a productive agricultural region, noted for growing apples, pears, and hops. In the 1930s, Yakima County was fifth out of all the counties in the U.S. for total agricultural production. The name Yakima originates from the Yakima Nation Native American tribe, whose reservation is located south of the city.

In 1941 just prior to World War II military units began using the Yakima Anti-Artillery Range for range firing and small unit training. From 1942 to 1946 the U.S. Army leased 160,000 acres for the Yakima Anti-Artillery Range. Currently artillery units from the Canadian Armed Forces based in British Columbia, as well as, the Japan Ground Self Defense Force conduct annual training in Yakima.

Buckingham Apartments
211 South Naches
Yakima, Washington

Yakima
Thursday

Dear Mother and all:

I am still here in Yakima. Have a pretty good job now. make about 20 to 25 a week but it is awful hard work. I have been so tired that I go to bed about 8:00. I am working in a warehouse piling pears. It is a large place [...] 250 carloads. [...]

[envelope overlaid:]
Mrs Earl Margrave
716 So 7th Av
Yakima
Wash.

Gordon
Neb.

YAKIMA AUG 12 12 M 1940 WASH.

Very good letter

[...] apples. John [...] my pears. [...] besides [...] a lot larger. They are worth about $45 a ton for 1st grade and $40 for second grade pears. [...] quit his job because he refused

August 12th 1940

Yakima, Washington

Dear Mother and All,

I am still here in Yakima. I have a pretty good job now. I make about 20 to 25 dollars a week, but it is awful hard work. I have been so tired that I go to bed about 8:00pm.

I am working in a warehouse piling pears. It is a large place that holds about 250 carloads. One thing about it is that you don't sweat much because it is about two degrees above freezing all the time. After I get hardened in it won't be so bad. It will last quite a while. After the pears comes the apples. I didn't think that there were so many pears. There are probably 20 other warehouses besides the one I work at and some a lot larger. They are worth about $25 a ton for first grade and $10 for second grade pears.

Spann quit his job because he refused to join the union. He went to Seattle a few days ago and I haven't heard from him since. If he gets a good job I am going over there. I worked with a fellow from Ainsworth that said he was a brother in law to Cliff Coz.

I guess I have gotten all of your letters and the ten bucks came in awful handy. If this draft bill is put across I'll be home before I have to go to the Army. I think that due to age I will be one of the first ones to serve. I am not going to worry about that until the time comes.

Tell Dad that there should be 289 head of cattle including the milk cows and upside down toadstool brand. That is counting the two Jim Grants and minus the cancer eye. 289 total.

Zentmires just trust me like a son.

Virgil makes about $250 a month working for Montgomery Ward. He said the first winter they were here they had to borrow on their car to get enough to eat.

I am going to a baseball game tonight.

Write.

As Ever,
Dwight M.

> "Spann quit his job **because he refused** to join the union."

August 29th 1940

Yakima, Washington

Dear Mother and all,

It is about time to write but I don't have much to say. I had a bad cold last week and I had to lay off a few days but I recovered. I got laid off the first of this week and so I am still looking for a job. I heard from a civil service job that I applied for and they sent me some more questions to answer. It is a dairy job, assistant manager of a dairy herd in a prison. It would really be a good job if I could get it. They might send you anyplace in the U.S. and pays $2,100 a year.

If Dad gets any letters from the Civil Service commission wanting to know how large a dairy herd I took care of, tell them 50 head. Zentmire is helping me to get a job on a Montgomery Ward truck. I may get that in about a week. It would be a pretty good job.

The Hop harvest is in full swing out here. There are about 20,000 Indians and bums picking this Valley. They get two cents a pound and a tent to live in, and make a dollar or two a day. The peaches and pears are about all gone. Peaches sold for 25¢ an apple box, real big fine peaches. It won't be long until apple season. I will try to send you a box of red delicious, some of the big ones.

I went to a 125-mile stock car race. A Graham came in first and Ford second and third. They couldn't keep their Fords or Mercury's cool. Five of them burnt out the bearings. There was only one car upset.

There are about 50 cases of Sleeping Sickness around here and about one out of every four people that get it die. Spann has been over in Seattle for the last two weeks trying to find a job. I haven't heard from him and I don't know whether he has one yet or not.

Write and tell me all about the County Fair.

Love,
Dwight Margrave

P.S. Oh is your Star Border back?
"Wally"

"I went to a 125-mile stock car race. A Graham came in first and Ford second and third."

Yakima Wash.
Aug. 29 –

Dear Mother and all,

It is about time to write but don't have much to say. Had a cold last week and had to lay off a day but I recovered. Got layed off the first of this week and so I am looking for a job. I heard from a civil service job the [?] and they [?]

[envelope:]
YAKIMA
AUG 29
5 PM
1940
WASH.

Mrs Earl Morgan
Gordon
Nebr.

SEATTLE

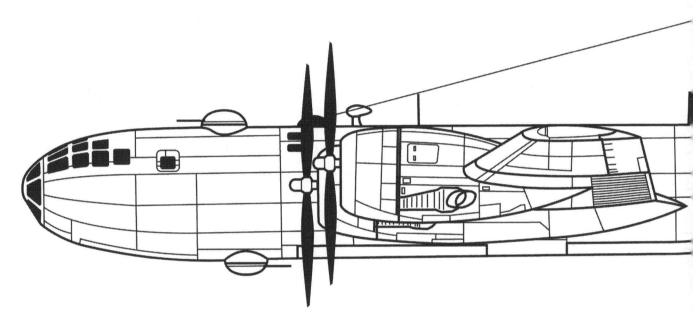

Circa 1940

Seattle is located on Puget Sound and was Washington State's largest city. The Great Depression was very hard on Seattle. During the 1934 Maritime Strike, Seattle lost most of its Asian trade to Los Angeles.

The Boeing Airplane Company was founded by William E. Boeing (1881-1956). Boeing was a major company in Seattle in 1940 and 1941, but it was not until the beginning of World War II that Boeing became the city's largest employer. The attack on Pearl Harbor in 1941 sparked an unprecedented explosion in Washington's aviation industry.

WASHINGTON

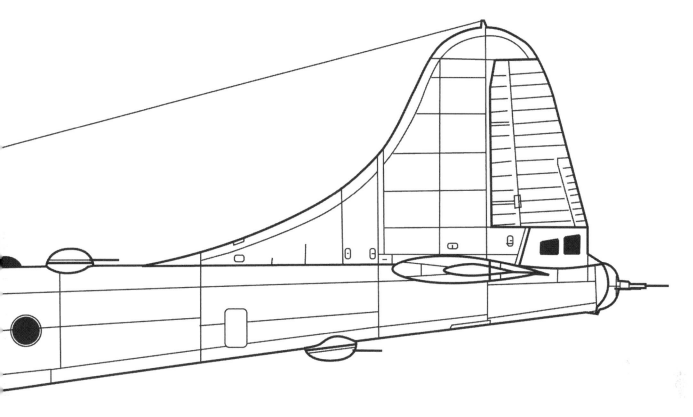

Boeing B-29 SUPER-FORTRESS

The company's Duwamish River complex in South Seattle was covered with camouflage netting so that hostile eyes could not see what was happening below. Tens of thousands of workers were feverishly building thousands of airplanes, including two of the most famous American aircraft of the war, the B-17 Flying Fortress and the B-29 Super Fortress.

September 26th 1940

Seattle, Washington

#3

Dear Mother and Dad and all:

Well I am OK. I have a job working in the mail order department of Sears Roebuck and Co. It doesn't pay so very much, 46½¢ per hour, but a steady job 44 hours per week and not such awful hard work. Spann could have had three different jobs on ships as fireman at about $100 a month but wouldn't take them because he did not want to go to Alaska
or China or somewhere. I think he will get a job tomorrow as pantry man at a hospital.

I heard from my Civil Service application today and had to get an identification picture and take an examination. I think I did pretty good in the examination. As I went to the city library ad got some books to "kinda brush up". I would sure like to get the job.
It pays $2,000 per year.

They are having a lot of traffic out at Boeing. Some of the men claim the Nazis run it.

We are staying with Ray Felix. They just took us in like lost sons. Ray works at Boeing. Norman's brother helped them get a job at the Coulee Dam and so they want to return the favor I guess.

I went fishing in the ocean and got a perch and a sea bass. They both weigh about three pounds. I just went down and sat on the dock when the tide was high. The tide raises
the water level about 12 feet here.

I almost got a job as a steward on an army transport that was going to Alaska and then
to the Hawaiian Islands. But they didn't think I had enough experience. I told them I had worked in a restaurant for six months. I would of sure liked to have had that job.

They are sure digging up lots of old ships that are all rusty and haven't been used for years and reconditioning them for Army or Navy transports. Nobody seems to know where they come from, just hid out from World War I days.

How is Marge and Marian getting along? This is a swell country. Things never get hot or much more than freezing in the winter.

It looks like the U.S. is just the same as in war. If I am drafted I will be home first. Those cows and calves had ought to be worth lots of money after while.

It has been foggy all day and rained this evening. There was some lightening which is very uncommon here. The people talk about it and admire the beauty of it.

There is an open call for 500 carpenters to go to Alaska but they must be journeymen at $1.50 per hour building airbases. Must Close.

Love,
Dwight Margrave

P.S. Tell Wally I bet he lost or loses his first two games.

"*They are having a lot of traffic out at Boeing. Some of the men claim the Nazis run it.*"

AS EVER, *Dwight*

#4

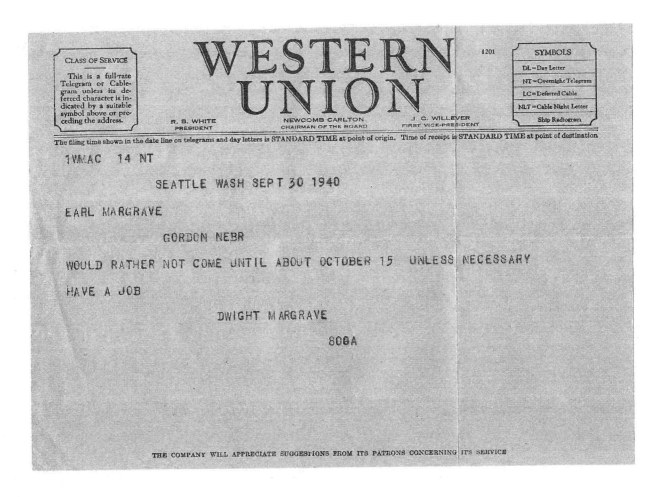

Top: Dwight informing his parents: "HAVE A JOB."

Right: Civil Service Application, Identification Picture September 1940.

Oct 7 - 40
3016½ 60 S[?]
Seattle

Dear Folks —

Well I am getting along O.K. only I don't know what to do about this draft. I think I would be better off if I would enlist before am drafted. what do you think If I join the navy I would have to stay for six years and that is too long. I would be [better] off to sell my car out [here] [because] [it] is worth a [$]20 more [here] [than ...] be at [...]
[...] have
[...] to leave
[...] and ho[me]
[...]
[...] beca[use]
[...] how he
[...] [proba]bly have
[...] in a sh[ip]
[...] lots of navy
[...] here, about 16 or twenty h[ave]
to go from the place I work

[Envelope:]
Mackerell Letters
Mrs Earl M[ackerell]
Gordon
Nebr.

SEATTLE, WASH.
OCT 8 10 PM 1940
TERMINAL ANNEX

October 7th 1940

Seattle, Washington

Dear Folks,

Well I am getting along OK only I don't know what to do about this draft. Think I would be better off if I would enlist before I am drafted. What do you think?

If I join the navy I would have to stay for six years and that is too long. I would be better off to sell my car out here. It is worth about $100 more than it would be at Gordon.

I think I had better come home this weekend although I hate to leave here because I like it out here and have a pretty good job.

Spann has been laughing because I will be conscripted and now he finds out that he will probably have to go back in the Navy in a short while. They are taking lots of navy reserves from here; about 15 or twenty have to go from the place I work, in the next week.

There is a big Greek ship out here that has been setting in the sound for two or three weeks. The crew is composed of Swedes, Japs, Germans and Norwegians and Greeks. They are on strike and won't sail because they don't want to leave this country and the authorities here won't let them go to shore because they aren't citizens. So I don't know what the outcome will be. It is loaded with scrap iron for Japan. Ships go out of here every day loaded with scrap iron going to Japan.

I have got to tell you a good one on me. When I was coming home from work the other night I dozed off to sleep. The motorman on the car woke me up at the end of the car line and asked me where I wanted off. I slept right on past the street where I was supposed to get off and had to take another car back about 40 blocks.

I sure felt foolish.

You will probably see me soon.

Love,
Dwight Margrave

> *"Think I would be better off if I enlist before I am drafted. What do you think?"*

1941 CHANGED EVERYTHING

Pearl Harbor: three stricken U.S. battleships. Left to right: U.S.S. West Virginia, severely damaged; U.S.S. Tennessee, damaged; and U.S.S. Arizona, sunk, December 7, 1941.

Friday

Dear folks — Aunt Alf
arrived here yesterday
didn't have any
trouble. Looked for
a job sunday but
havent run on to any
thing yet. I talked
to my boss in Sears
and he said to go see
the manager and I would
probably go to work
but I think I will look
for something — Aubrey
2947-42th

June 7th 1941
Seattle, Washington

Dear Folks and all,

Arrived here yesterday. I didn't have any trouble. I looked around for a job some but I haven't run onto anything yet.

I talked to Rudy's boss in Sears and he said to go see the manager and I could probably go to work but I think I will look around first.

My address is:
2747 47th S.W.,
Seattle, Washington.

Love,
Dwight

AS EVER, *Dwight*

June 13th 1941

Seattle, Washington

#7

Dear Folks,

Thought I would put off writing until I could write to you and tell you about the job I have. It pays 90¢ per hour, 56 hours per week. But guess where? It is at the Army Air Base at Anchorage, Alaska. I have had my physical exam and vaccine shots for typhoid and small pox. The boats are leaving the 19th and the 21st of the month. The only drawback is that it costs you $2.20 per day for board and room. You get free passage and meals on the way up and back if you stay six for months.

There is only one thing that might keep me from going and that is the draft board. But the War Department wrote them a letter yesterday and asked them to give me a six months traveling permit, which they will probably do. Bob Zentmire is going also.

Spann had a day off so we drove over here to Yakima today as he wanted to come. He is getting along fine and on the 15th he gets another raise in pay which will make him about $1.75 per hour I think. I am just going up as a laborer but I understand they are going to reclassify the men up there and some will get more pay. The job will net about $35 per week and board and room and laundry.

I am going to sell my car or trade it off for a new one when I come back. In other words I will trade it off now and take delivery on return. Sporvn said he would buy it if I couldn't do anything else.

Well what do you think of that job? How were the races? How is Marion? She is riding horseback no doubt.

The Zentmires aren't doing so good. I guess Virgil got his pay cut about half and so he quit and now he is talking about going to Alaska. Everyone I have talked with that has been there says the climate isn't so bad at Anchorage, although it gets minus 10 degrees in the winter.

Write and tell me what you think of it. I won't leave before the 21st I don't think.

Love,
Dwight M.

P.S. Today is my 25th birthday.

> "*...only one thing **that might keep me from going** and that is the draft board.*"

Dwight heading north to Alaska in search of work, 1941.

FORT RICHARDSON

Circa 1941

Fort Richardson was built during 1940-1941. It's adjacent to the city of Anchorage, Alaska. The fort encompasses 84,000 acres, which includes space for offices, family housing, a heliport, a drop zone suitable for airborne and air-land operations, firing ranges, and other training areas.

Nearby mountain ranges offered soldiers the opportunity to learn mountain glacier warfare and rescue techniques. Fort Richardson Army Base is headquarters to the United States Army Alaska. It is one of the United States Army Pacific Command units.

Alaska

July 29

Dear Folks;

P.S. — 2 frogs Ice here the other nite

Received your letter a few "5" days after it was mailed and sure glad to get it. They get here pretty fast by Air but it takes about 2 w by boat. Boats come into Seward about every day as th t have to come over here by rail. Am getting a li ore information about the country now. This R.R. t mes through here goes to Fairbanks 470 miles from S d i Right Maryur three days. It crosses it own track b etw 706 S. Army Engineers I don't know how many t tu Hdq. Richardson a highway f alo Anchorage Alaska ke. A

Mrs Earl Margrave
Gordon
Nebraska

ANCHORAGE, ALASKA
UL 6-PM 1941

U.S. POSTAGE VIA AIR MAIL 6¢

plan miles to pal uska V la in a co there would like to go I trains upshore about 4 ast have but it lucky only 1 shift and I have t

July 29th 1941

U.S. Army Engineers
Fort Richardson, Anchorage, Alaska

Dear Folks:

Received your letter five days after it was mailed and I was sure glad to get it. They get here pretty fast by airmail but it takes about three weeks by boat. Boats come into Seward about every day or two but then they have to come over here by rail.

I am getting a little more information about the country now. The Frisco Railroad comes through here and goes to Fairbanks. It is 470 miles from Seward and it takes two or three days. It crosses it's own track six times between here and Fairbanks.

There is a highway from Valdez to Fairbanks, but I don't know what it is like.

To get to Nome you have to fly, walk, or go by boat. A plane ticket costs about $60 from here. It is about 450 miles. There is about 75 miles of highway here that goes to Palmer, the closest town. It is a little place in the Madawaska Valley where they sent the Swedes up from Minnesota in a colony a few years back.

They have a bumper crop up there this year. Potatoes are produced about four to six tons per acre and sell for $2.75 per hundred; so I guess they are making money. I would like to go up and look it over sometime.

It rains up here about four times per week but I have hit it lucky, only one shift in the rain and I have put in 25 shifts. Time sure goes by fast, but working eight hours a day, seven days a week: it makes you want to take a day off. If I don't miss any for a year I get 30 days with pay and transportation to the States.

I got my furlough but it is only good to the 20th of December '41.

Now, about the questions you ask: the meat comes from Swift in Chicago or Omaha. I think it is all frozen and I believe first grade. We have bacon and sausage for breakfast, cereal, sometimes grapefruit and oranges, prunes, cakes, potatoes, eggs, toast and coffee. For dinner we get beef or fish, potatoes, bread, and vegetables; both fresh and canned, and pie. For supper we get fried pork or beef, potatoes, cakes, etc.

AS EVER, *Dwight*

You don't need a rope to keep the snakes out of your bed as there aren't any in Alaska. Set up in a tent for a while and now I have moved in to a bunkhouse.

There is the biggest and best Ford dealer in the west coast here and has been here for 25 years. I went to a bank and asked about them and they said they were OK.

We had one good clear day the other day and you could see the Alaska Range of mountains and Mt. McKinley, about 75 miles away. It is the highest mountain in North America at 20,000 plus feet. I would like to take a month off and go prospecting inland. They fly away and bring them supplies or pick them up every so often. A fellow showed me a pocket full of nuggets, about like this <............> big.

The Salmon run is on now. They are catching silvers up to 30 pounds just a half mile from camp. I got two that weighed about 15 to 20 pounds. There is nothing to do with them after you catch them but to throw them back in the creek. Tell Mort that they pay a bounty of ten cents apiece on trout. They do pay two cents per tail on Dolly Varden trout in certain places because they eat the Salmon eggs. There is everything from rats, beaver, bear, and wolves to trap.

It looks to me like the cattle price will continue to be good for another year or two as this thing hasn't even started yet. They have 10,000 soldiers here at Fort Richardson now and are building 100 new two story barracks.

Sincerely,

Your Son
Dwight E. Margrave

P.S. It froze ice here the other night.

> *"I would like to take a month off and go prospecting inland. A fellow showed me a pocket full of nuggets."*

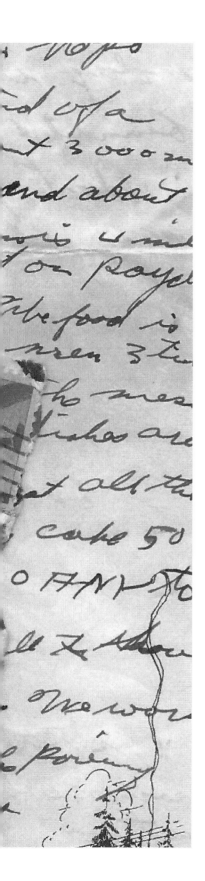

ANDERSON CAMP

Circa 1941

Anderson Camp, Anchorage Alaska was a Civilian Conservation Corp (CCC) camp. The Camp ceased operation in April 1942 because the CCC had been disbanded with the coming of war in December 1941. Then the camp was briefly used as a training base for the 10th Army Air Force Rescue Boat Squadron that was training in Ketchikan, Alaska.

The (CCC) was launched by President Franklin D. Roosevelt in April 1933 as a relief to the great depression sweeping across America.

The CCC was a voluntary public work relief program that operated from 1933-1942 in the United States for unemployed, unmarried men. Originally for young men ages 18-25 it was eventually expanded to ages 17-26.

August 4th 1941

Anderson Camp
Anchorage, Alaska

#9

Dear Sis,

Thought I would drop you a line in hopes that I might get a letter back. It is a kind of a lonesome place up here. There are about three thousand men working here on the airport and barracks, and about ten thousand soldiers here at Fort Richardson. The town is four miles from here and about six thousand residents. You should see it on payday. There are about two thousand men staying here in this camp.

The food is good, but when they have to feed that many men three times a day you can imagine what it is like in the mess hall. The men just gobble up the eats, slam dishes around and somebody is shouting for more coffee or meat all of the time. It's just like those old cows eating cake. Five hundred people can eat at one time.

I work from 3:30am - 12:00pm with a ½ hour lunch break. It's awful to have to get up at that time in the morning. We work seven days a week.

I am working with the paving gang pulling forms after the concrete is set. We have about one hundred acres paved already. I don't have to work so very hard, and the last three days we have been out of cement and haven't had any thing to do, only fool around. But we still get our $7.20.

We use eighteen thousand bags of cement in twenty four hours in our mixer and there are two of them. There are lots of Army planes to watch up here, Fighters and Bombers.

We had an earthquake the other day. It shook the hell out of things. Two men have been killed from falling off of the hangers that are being built since I have been here, and one man was terribly hurt.

We go down to the River about one half of a mile and catch all of the salmon we want to. We catch five to twenty pound salmons, and then just throw them back in the river. There is nothing else to do with them.

I sure had a swell boat ride up here. It took us six days. We went on the inside passage and it was the most beautiful scenery I have ever seen. I don't get much news, only what is in the paper and it is about like the Gordon Journal or something like that. I am sending a clipping that is a good one.

I have never met anyone that I knew since I left Seattle. I don't know much more to write.

Your Brother,
Dwight M.

P.S. X on the map, marks where I am at.

Alaska

Anchorage, Alaska
Aug 4 – 41

Dear Leo,-

Thought I would drop you a line in hopes that I might get a letter as it is a kind of a lonesome place up here. There is about 3000 men working here on the airport and Barracks and about 2000 there at Ft. Richardson. The town is 4 miles

[envelope addressed to:]
Miss Marjorie Margrave
℅ J H L Ranch
Ashby,
Nebraska

VIA AIR MAIL
ANCHORAGE, ALASKA
1—PM AUG 5 1941

...This camp. The food is...men 3 ti...the mess...dishes a...at all th...cake 50...

...days a week...pulling forms after the con...have about 700 acres poured already...have to work so very hard and the...3 days we have been out of cement and haven't...

Dwight would send home news clippings
from the Anchorage Daily Times.

ASKA, SATURDAY, AUGUST 2, 1941

IDEA WORKS TOO WELL AND BRUIN TREES PVT. SANDERS

Pvt. Ray Sanders of the Infantry had a little bear trouble while on duty at one of the outposts. There is a 400 pound black bear that roams around near the camp and feeds on the waste left by the kitchen, so Sanders decided that he would take his picture climbing a tree. He placed a piece of bacon on the trunk about ten feet up from the base and then climbed above the bacon, so as to get a picture, looking down at the bear.

All went well. The bear climbed the tree, got the bacon and Sanders got the picture. The bear took the bacon to the bottom of the tree where he proceeded to take his time eating it. All this time, Sanders remained in the tree.

After the bear had finished the bacon he started up the tree again. Sanders wasn't quite sure whether the bear was after more bacon or him. About that time, Sanders proved his heritage and out-climbed the bear foot for foot, all the time hollering bloody murder. One of the other fellows at the camp, hearing the disturbance, threw another piece of bacon at the bear. "Bruin" preferring the bacon to Sanders, came down out of the tree and took home the bacon.

Ocean Dock Ready for Use

Wants to Tax Union

Carl Margrave
Gordon
Nebraska

ANCHORAGE, ALASKA
6 PM
AUG 28
1941

August 27th 1941

Anderson Camp
Anchorage, Alaska

Dear Folks,

I received the shirt and it fits okay. It sure is a dandy – thank you. I have been working the same shift, 3:30am to 12:00pm. I have not missed a shift or been late yet. The job is getting pretty well finished for this year. The runways are completed and the hangers are about finished. Some of the men have been transferred to another base at Seward. I could have gone down there but I didn't.

We have had awful good weather for about two weeks with no rain. I may get transferred to another base at Dutch Harbor or Kodiak.

They are both Navy Air Stations. There are union jobs but; they said they thought they could transfer men from the Army Engineer to the Navy Bases someway. It pays a little more money but the weather is awful tough. It doesn't get much below freezing but lots of wind rain and snow. The snow melts about as soon as it falls.

I think we get Labor Day off. I may go to the Matanuska Valley where they are having a fair. I don't care so much for the fair but would like to see the country. It is where the Swedes from Minnesota were sent up there in a colony in 1934. They say that they have cabbage that weights 40 pounds to the head. It is a very short growing season but the sun shines nearly 24 hours a day in the summer.

I may take a plane up there. It costs only four or five dollars to fly there. By comparison it costs about three dollars on the railroad for fifty miles. I have established a bank account and I have a little money in it.

A fellow here that I have gotten acquainted with wants me to go back to the States with him in about a month. He is from Los Angeles. He says he can get me in the Union there and will break me in with him as a steel worker. He seems to know his stuff about steel work. I think I could do the work if I had a chance to break in. There is a big demand for steel workers now. They can go to work anyplace. He makes $85 a week here and the scale is a $1.50 per hour in the States. He is working here on the base for a contractor that is installing and building the power plant for the base.

"I received the shirt and it fits okay. It's sure a dandy – thank you."

They have about four hundred men working and will be finished with the steel soon. Then they can go to work in Texas, the Philippines or Hawaii for the same company where they have other defense contracts. It sounds like a good chance to get a trade and I wouldn't have much to lose. When you write to me tell me what you think about it.

Are the calves eating oats? Does Marjorie have a school? Is Marion going to school? I think she should. Does Mom's chickens still bother the Cases? Does Dad still go to bed early and get up early? I think I can beat him both ways since I have worked this shift. I got up at 2:45am this morning.

Love to all,
Dwight Margrave

P.S. I went to some prize fights last night.
The referees covering it got hit by the boxers,
and maybe half dozen fights broke out in the crowd.
It was a fierce slugging bunch.

Dwight with his new shirt at Anderson Camp, Anchorage, Alaska 1941.

September 9th 1941
Anderson Camp
Anchorage, Alaska

#11

Mother,

Please send my winter underwear and those heavy wool socks.

Don't send it airmail as it will cost too much just parcel post. They want from $3.50 to $8.00 for a suit of long underwear up here.

Dwight

Mother —

Please send my winter underwear, and those heavy wool sox. Don't send it Airmail it will cost twice as much just Parcel post.

They want from $3.50 to $8.00 a suit for underwear up here —

Dwight

September 13th 1941

Anderson Camp
Anchorage, Alaska

#12

Dear Folks,

Just got your letter and the present. It sure is a nice ring.

Well, I guess I won't leave with that fellow from LA as I have a job coming up here soon at $12 a day seven days a week; if something doesn't go haywire. It is running a Caterpillar and a Le Tourneau like they had on the road south of Gordon. I talked to the boss and he tried me out on one and I got along o.k., but have to wait until there is an opening. It shouldn't be long as there is about thirty or forty men quitting every day.

We had a hard freeze last night and probably snow soon they say. Then there will be a lot more leaving.

I am getting kind of tired of staying here myself but if I get this better job I know I will like it.

The worst of it is you work every day and don't get to go any place only to town. We had labor day off and I went to Palmer the only day I had off since I have been here.

Those calves sure weighed good; but it is a little early to sell calves isn't it? It might be a good thing to keep some of those cows if you can find a place to keep them.

I have gotten two of the Gordon papers but I didn't find anything in them worthwhile reading.

I have been here about two and one half months and I have about $200 in the bank. It is not quite as good as I figured but not so bad. I haven't had any hard work to do here lately. We work just about like a WPA gang. I didn't get many good pictures but I am sending what I got on the way up.

Send me Marion's address and I will write to her when she gets to school. I just heard today that they are going to transfer men from here to Kodiak and Dutch Harbor. Some friends of mine killed a moose and a bear; so I am going to eat moose meat with them. The big game season opened the 1st of September. There are lots of moose and bear, mountain sheep and caribou.

Your Son,
Dwight E. Margrave

DWIGHT EARL MARGRAVE
A SOLDIER'S JOURNEY THROUGH WWII

"*Getting kind of tired of staying here, **but if I get this better job I know I'll like it.***"

Dear Folks—

Just a short line to let you know I am OK. I got a raise in pay about the [...] 1.10 p/hr. Makes me $8.8[...]

Carl Morgan
Gordon

September 25th 1941

Anderson Camp
Anchorage, Alaska

Dear Folks,

Just a short line to let you know that I am OK. I will get a raise in pay about the 27th. At a $1.10 per hour, I make $8.80 a day.

I am going to run a caterpillar in about a week or two. I will go on steady at $1.50 per hour, or $12 a day. That will really count up to $360 per month.

I started working from 12:00pm until 8:00pm today. It is not a bad shift although it gets dark at 6:00pm.

I burned my hand on some hot tar the other day. It is not serious but I had to go the first aid station. They treat you like babies around here.

If you get a scratch and the blood shows, you have to go to the first aid station and get it dressed.

Well, I must get ready and go to work.

Love,
Dwight Margrave

"I burned my hand on some hot tar the other day... I had to go the first aid station. They treat you like babies around here."

AS EVER, *Dwight*

September 28th 1941

Anderson Camp
Anchorage, Alaska

#14

Dear Folks,

This is terrible country. There is a foot of frost in the ground and eight inches of snow on top of that. We had our first snow last night. It must have been about zero. It hasn't been so very cold here but it hasn't thawed any for about two weeks. It just snows to stay below freezing.

I bought me some heavy clothes so I am fairing pretty well. My job on the cat played out; because the ground is frozen so hard. They are cutting down to one shift and that left me out.

I went over to another crew. I am on the mechanics crew. Helpers get $1.00 per hour. I work on the gas truck from 4:00pm to midnight. Not a very good shift but an easy job. There is only part of the men working on Sundays now, but I am still on seven days a week.

Dad how did those cows and calves sell? And how did you come out on the ones that you bought? Cattle must be awful high now. I kinda hated to see those cows go. They were a pretty good bunch but it is probably a high time to sell them now.

I don't have much to write about; I haven't been any place or done anything. I went down to a cabin with a couple of boys I know yesterday and had a big feed of moose steak. It is good meat, it tastes about like beef. They bought this from some fellow for twenty five cents a pound. That is cheap for meat in this country. Beef steak is about 50 cents a pound, cold storage eggs, 55 cents a dozen and fresh eggs a dollar a dozen if you can get them.

I have had a cold, but I am feeling fine now.

Your son,
Dwight E. Margrave

"My job on the Caterpillar played out; because the ground is frozen."

Alaska

Dear Folks, 9-23-41

This is a terrible country. Lots of fog in the ground and inches of snow and that. We had our first snow last month of been about zero & hasent been above my cabin here but, but it hasnt it has my pen about two weeks of just freezes day below freezing. I bought me some clothes too I am fairing pretty well. My job on the cat played out since the ground is froze so hard they are cutting down to one shift and that is down out but I went onto another job I am on the ___ ___ ___ get 1.40

Alaska

Oct. 8 – 1941

Dear Mother & Dad –

Received your letter yesterday and it was mailed Sept 26 – not very good mail service. I'm still working driving a cat, for the last four days I have been in the base hanger on some 60 ft. towers that the painters use to stand on to paint the cealing, it is a pretty good job although it is chilly and a draft blows through there no windows or doors in there. I don't know if I am getting $1.50 an hour yet or probably not. The men are sure quitting, Kay Albert left. They tried to hire 50 painters at 1.50 per and only got two. For a while there was 500 men eating here at the camp and now there is only about 600. They are going to start drafting men from Alaska into the Army just the same as back in the states

October 8th 1941

Anderson Camp
Anchorage, Alaska

Dear Mother and Dad,

Received your letter yesterday and it was mailed Sept. 26th – not very good mail service. I am still working driving a Cat. The last four days I have been in the base hanger moving some 60 feet towers that the painters used to stand on to the paint the ceiling. It is a pretty soft job although it is chilly and a draft blows through. There are no windows or doors yet.

I don't know if I am getting $1.50 an hour yet or not, probably not. The men are sure quitting. Kip Albertson left. They tried to hire 50 painters at $1.50 per hour and only got two. For awhile there were 1,500 men eating here at the camp and now there are only about 600.

They are going to start drafting men from Alaska into the Army just the same as back in the States. The first ones go the 15th. They will be sent here for training. I knew some of them that were working here on the base and were the first ones on the list. They all caught a boat and left for the States, permission or not they said. They were going to get out of this country if they had to go to the Army.

It is sure a pretty tough life being a soldier up here. They have had soldiers here for about 18 months and 80 of them have gone crazy and about ten have committed suicide and quite a few have deserted.

Mom, I wrote once and told you I got the ring. There isn't much to tell you about this town, only that it is just a boom town full of bars. Very few boats come up here because of the tide. It is the fastest tide in the world and the next highest, 35 feet. The water is too shallow to have a good dock. When the tide goes out the boats have to go to the deepest water or they are grounded.

The snow comes down a little further on the mountains every time it rains but we haven't had any here yet. The mountains were all bare but the tops and now they are covered clear to the foot hills. Tell Walt that there are lots of duck, geese, ptarmigan and grouse (blue), moose, caribou, reindeer, black bear, brown bear, grizzly bear, and I'm thinking Kodiak bear.

A bomber wrecked on the landing field the other day but didn't hurt any one.

Your son,
Dwight M.

AS EVER, *Dwight*

October 18th 1941

Anderson Camp
Anchorage, Alaska

#16

Dear Folks,

Just got the package you sent yesterday, thank you. Good pictures. The candy was dried out and it was hard to chew, but tasted good.

It has been about zero here for two weeks, but no wind and not much snow, although it is snowing right now. I have been working inside which is not so bad in this kind of weather as it doesn't warm up in the day time. The sun doesn't come up until 9:00am and sets about 3:00pm. This makes a pretty short day.

We got Armistice Day off with pay, and will get Thanksgiving Day off also. I have had only five days off since I have been here. Two holidays and two Sundays. I was laid off one day when I had that cold, but I am feeling fine now.

My roommate flew to Fairbanks and isn't back. He worked for some fellow up there for a year and didn't get any wages. He is trying to collect them in court. He is from Mississippi and has been in Alaska for six years.

I met a fellow here that used to live up at Albany Nebraska in about 1908. His name is Robinson. He asked me to find out what township and range Albany was in, as he needed that information to get a birth certificate. He said he wrote to Rushville, but received no answer. I thought Dad would probably know.

Dad, if you buy any of that land... Buy it cheap!

I know one fellow that has a brother that leases an Island from the Government for $50.00 per year. It is about four miles long and three miles wide and it never gets to zero there.

He raises firs, foxes, etc. Others lease these islands and raise sheep.

How would you like to have a ranch like that? There would be no wind mills or salt to buy. There would be no gates to be left open, or no trespassers. There would be plenty of driftwood to burn. But it would be a thousand miles from a town, and then maybe it's not such a good thing after all.

Must close,
Dwight M.

Oct 7 Tues 41

Dear Folks —

Just got the package you sent
today. Thanks you, good pr[...]
candy was dried out — til
was hard to chew but tas[ted]
[good]
[It] has been about zero here [for]
[two] weeks but no wind and no
snow although it is throw[ing]
[a few flakes?] Have been working inside [so]
it is not so bad this kind [of]
[weath]er as it don't warm up in [the]
[day]time. The sun doesn't come up [un]-
till 9:00 and sets about 3:00 [so a]
[pre]tty short day. We get Arm[istice]
[Day] with pay and Thanksgiving [too]
I have only had 5 days off
[since I] have been here, two holidays a[nd two]
Sundays and layed off one day [when]
I had that cold — Future let[ter?]

D. Margraves
Anderson Camp
Anchorage, Alaska

UNITED STATES POSTAGE
3 CENTS

ANCHORAGE, ALASKA
NOV 21
3 PM
1941

VIA AIR

Nov 1-

Dear Folks-

Just got you letters today- it is the first Air Mail that has been in Anchorage for 15 days and there hasen't been any mail boats in for about 0 days so I guess no one has been getting any letters-

Well I transfered to another job again, sanding it isent hard and

November 21st 1941

Anderson Camp
Anchorage, Alaska

Dear Folks,

Just got your letters today. It is the first air mail that has been in Anchorage for fifteen days, and there hasn't been any mail boats in for about 10 days so I guess no one has been getting any letters.

Well, I transferred to another job again; sanding. It isn't so bad and it is supposed to pay $1.25 per hour. I didn't like working on the gas truck. The diesel oil would get on my clothes and make me sick.

The kid I used to bunk with here quit and went to another job at Portage Junction. He was up last week and showed me his check for last week, $162. That's pretty good for one weeks wages. He is a carpenter.

They had one of those mock wars here last week. The air raid, alarm blew and planes dived at the buildings.

I was coming home from work the other night and the sentry halted me and made me show my ID. card. It makes you nervous to have a 45 stuck in your ribs and some crazy soldier on the other end of it hoping he will get to shoot someone so he will get transferred out of Alaska.

I think the cattle sold for a good price. There was not any (brand) steer as you said you couldn't find one. But there was a dozen three year old (brand) heifers.

The people up here don't eat much beef. They eat lots of fish and they kill a moose for winter meat. Some of the moose weigh up to 1,800 pounds.

I will write to the draft board and see if I can get another deferment. I probably can't as there are men getting calls to go to the Army from here all the time. If I can't get one I think I will leave here the first of the year. My deferment expires on Christmas and that is not so far away. The fifth of January I will have six months in and be eligible for a 15 day vacation with pay.

I am going to get stuck paying for the school tax up here, five dollars for all men between 21 and 58 years old. Will close.

As Ever,
Dwight M.

DWIGHT EARL MARGRAVE
A SOLDIER'S JOURNEY THROUGH WWII

DEC 7th

PEARL HARBOR

"...we are at war for sure and it looks like it will be a long while before it is over."

Pearl Harbor: Battered by aerial bombs and torpedoes, the U.S.S. California is evacuated as sailors and soldiers look on, December 7, 1941.

AS EVER, *Dwight*

World War II, Pearl Harbor, Hawaii, the destruction of the USS West Virginia, December 7, 1941, official U.S. Navy photograph.

The wreckage of the destroyers USS Downes and USS Cassin at Pearl Harbor dry dock.

Anchorage
Dec 8, 19[41]

Dear Folks—

Guess we are at war [now]
and it looks like it will be [a]
while before it is over. Say [the]
army sure did move arou[nd]
yesterday and today, they loaded [up]
planes with bombs and too[k off]
I don't know where they wen[t]
Everything is blacked out ou[t]
here and in town and won't [be]
that [...]

Mrs Earl Morgan
Gordon
Nebraska

D Morgan
[...] Anderson Camp
Anchorage Alaska

ANCHORAGE, ALASKA
DEC 9
1 PM
1941

VIA AIR MA[IL]

December 8th 1941

Anderson Camp
Anchorage, Alaska

Dear Folks,

Guess we are at war for sure and it looks like it will be a long while before it is over. Say, the army sure did move around here yesterday and today. They loaded all the planes with bombs and took off. I don't know where they went. Everything is blacked out on the base here and in town. It will remain that way for an indefinite length of time. Air raid instructions were announced.

It has been from minus zero to minus 25° below zero for the last two or three weeks. The army had lots of trouble getting the trucks started yesterday. They kept the planes running all night. If those Japs come up here they will freeze to death, for sure.

I may get caught up here and not be able to get out. I don't know. So far as we know there will be two boats on the 12th. I just don't know whether to pull out and leave here or stay. I don't know if they will allow anyone to leave. I guess that I could fly out.

I am working for a different foreman now. I am a brick layer helper and it pays ten dollars a day. It isn't such a bad job. It is inside; which is sure lucky in this kind of weather.

Was sick last week. Had a cold and the flu, I guess. Missed four and one half days of work and didn't feel good for two or three more days, but am o.k. now.

We had a sixty mile an hour wind which blew for two days. One of the pursuit planes here was lost while in a power dive during the storm. The wings tore off of the plane and the wreckage went into the bay. They have never found it or the pilot. It was about the strongest wind I have ever seen.

We are safe here. There's only two ways the Japs could come in: by air or railroad and it isn't very likely that they will come in either way.

Write and let me know what you think, should I leave or stay?

I will not send any Christmas presents as they might not get there. Everything is so confused. I better not send any.

I will write again soon,
Dwight M.

AS EVER, *Dwight*

Anchorage
Dec 8, 1941,

Dear Folks —

Guess we are at war for sure and it looks like it will be a long while before it is over. Say, the army sure did move around here yesterday and today, they loaded all the planes with bombs and took off. I don't know where they went. Everything is blacked out on the base here and in town and will remain that way for an indefinite length of time. Airraid instructions were announced. It has been from -0 to -25 below 0 for the last two or three weeks. The army had lots of trouble getting the trucks all started yesterday and kept the planes running all nite. If those Japs come up here they will freeze to death sure —

I may get caught up here and not be able to get out, I don't know — so far as we know there will be two boats the 12th. I just don't know weather to

Complete letter from December 8th, 1941, after the bombing of Pearl Harbor.

pull out and leave here or stay and
I don't know if they will allow anyone to leave. I guess that I could fly out.

I am working for a different firm
now, am a brick layer helper, 10 a day
and it isent such a bad job, it is inside
which is sure luckey this kind of wether.

Was sick last week — had a cold
and the flu I guess, missed 4½ days
work and didn't feel good for 2 or three
more but am O.K. now. We had a 60
mile wind which blew for two days, one of the
persuit planes here was out while in
a power dive during the storm the wing
tore off the plane and the wreckage went
into the bay, they have never found it
or the pilot. It was about the strongest wind
I have ever seen.

We are safe here, there is only two ways
the Japs could come in, by air, or R.R. and
it isent very likely that they will come in either
way. But let me know what you think,
should I leave or stay. Will not send any
Christmas presents as they might not get
there, everything is so confused, better not send
any. Will write again soon.

Dwight M

Dec. 31 —

Dear Folks —

We are O.K. up here an[d]
haven't been bombed or any[thing]
The boats are getting through
I think, anyway we have plenty
everything to eat. They are [sending?]
the army men wives and ch[ildren]
out if [they want?] and they are [hearing?]
rumors that they are going to [send]
all base workers wives and a[ll?]
out unless they have been re[sidents?]
for five years or longer. We [are]
supposed to get gas masks in a [few]
days.

Everyone around here seems
a little bit nervous but I alon[g]

December 31st 1941

Anderson Camp, Anchorage, Alaska
(Letters examined by censor from this point)

Dear Folks,

We are o.k. up here and haven't been bombed or anything. The boats are getting through now. I think, anyway we have plenty of everything to eat. They are shipping the Army men's wives and children out of here and there are several rumors they are going to ship all base workers wives and dependents out unless they have been residents for five years or longer. We are supposed to get gas masks in a few days.

Everyone around here seems to be a little nervous but I don't think anyone is afraid of the Japs. The base here is getting pretty well completed unless they start to expanding it. The powerhouse is finished and the plan is to put in a temporary steam line into the base hangers tomorrow. We have it nearly completed except the floor has to be concrete and they ran out of window glass, but they put in plywood.

All of the glass is painted black everywhere. We are blacked out every night but the buses run in the dark just the same. Without flashlights it is sure dark. It has been slick here. It has been warm but not thawing until yesterday. We got a warm south wind and then it has been raining since then. It seems to make the snow just like ice. It is raining hard now. Am glad I am working inside. Did I tell you I am getting $1.25 per hour now? I am rated as a handyman working with the brick layers.

I got Christmas off with pay and they had a big feed here at camp. Wished I could have been at home. I got Dad's letter mailed the 16th but I never got the gloves. I got one Christmas card and it had been censored. That is all the mail I have had since the war broke out.

Dad must be hustling around buying and selling. It is interesting that you are just working for the government, and income tax will get it. They will get quite a cut out of me this year too. I think I could get out of here now but I don't know whether to go or stay. Write to me and let me know what you think about it.

As Ever, Happy New Year,
Dwight M.

P.S. Jan. 1st 1942, I just got your letter, it was censored and I believe I will stay here as long as possible now since I have heard from you. I had to work today. I can't send any pictures. It is dark most of the time. And you aren't allowed to have cameras on the base. There is something in the air up here, they are allowing men to quit now and I may be laid off. No one seems to know for sure. I will mail this now.

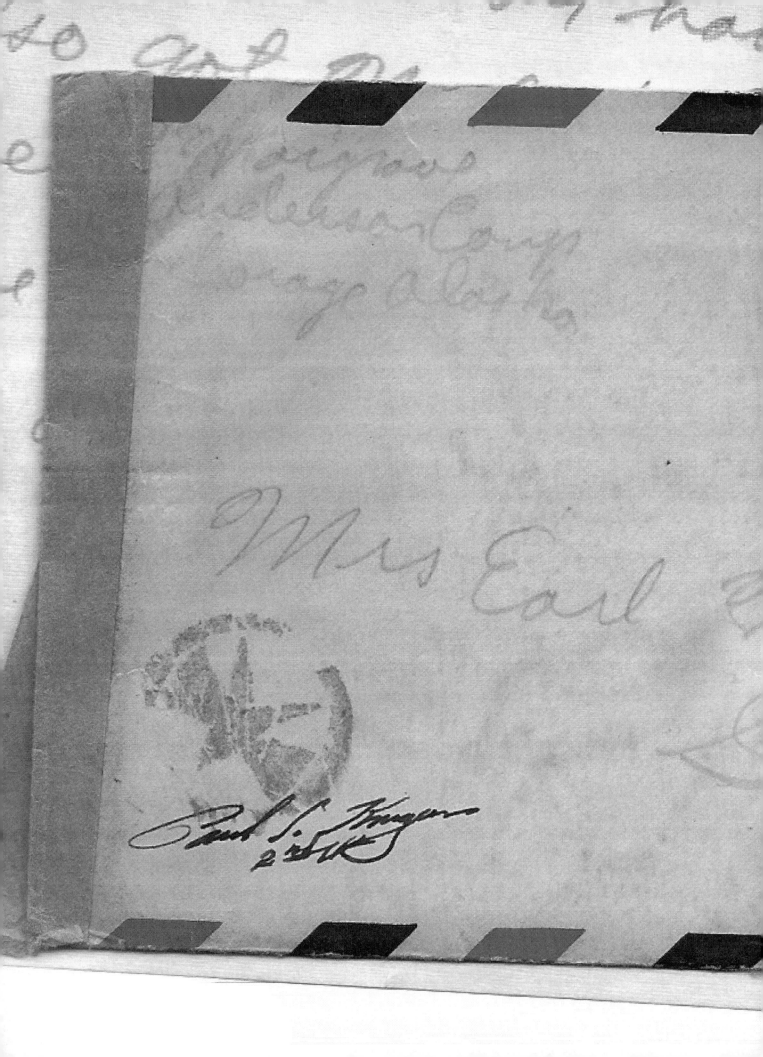

1942
WELCOME TO THE ARMY

AS EVER, *Dwight*

January 20th 1942

Anderson Camp
Anchorage, Alaska

#20

Dear Folks,

We are getting along just fine up here. The weather has been good. It has been raining every once in awhile. The days are getting longer; it makes you think spring is about here, although these black outs will eventually make you moon eyed I believe. We still go to work in the dark and come home in the dark.

They brought a sheet around the other day that we had to fill out giving our age and our draft board. Then the office will notify them that we are deferred until we are terminated from this job. And so I guess I am deferred until I leave here.

Just got your Christmas package the other day. I think that its a rather neat shaving bag. I never did get the gloves; I think they must have been lost in the mail.

I am not working today. I am going to town and get a tooth pulled. It is an upper wisdom tooth and it has been bothering me. I get paid for today just the same as if I had worked. I have seven days with pay coming now that I have six months in. Also have thirteen days vacation that I can take with pay but I think I will let the vacation go until I leave and then collect for it. It keeps adding up all the time at the rate of two days a month.

You don't need to worry about us getting bombed up here as we are really well protected. This is one place the Japs had better stay away from if they intend to keep alive.

Everything is terrible high up here; gas is 45¢ a gallon. There is a shortage of coal and fuel oil.

Dwight M.

"I never did get the gloves; I think they must have been lost in the mail."

...are getting longer makes
...ing is about here. Although
...outs will evid eventu...
...moon eyed I believe.
...ark and co...

...ngraw
...erson Camp
...age Alaska

and

Mrs Earl Mangraw
Gordon
Nebraska

ANCHORAGE, ALASKA
JAN 20
6 PM
1942

VIA AIR MAIL

...o I guess I am...

Feb 5- 47

Dear folks-

Dont have much to write about have been working every day and get pretty well along - Lots of things to write about but we have had orders on what to write and what not to.

Could of went to work on another job at Nackmic, over on the bearing sea, but didn't go, I think I could of have made about $450 a month on a cat for a couple of months. They fly you in and back out-

Two planes crashed up here the other day 9 in one plane and one killed the fellow in the other plane parachuted out

The weather has been good not much snow and not very cold but it doesn't thaw any either.

February 5th 1942

Anderson Camp
Anchorage, Alaska
Insert: Newspaper clipping, The Kayototokyo Club

Dear Folks,

Don't have much to write about. I have been working every day and getting along pretty well. There are lots of things to write about but we have had orders on what to write and what not to.

I could have gone to work on another job at Naknek over in the Bering Sea but I didn't go, I think I could have made about $450 per month on a cat for a couple of months. They fly you in and back out.

Two planes crashed the other day. Nine in one plane and one was killed, the fellow in the other plane parachuted out.

The weather has been good not much snow and not very cold but it doesn't thaw any either. The days are long enough that we go to work in the day and quit before dark now. It makes you think spring should be here soon.

Dad, how would you like to go 50/50 on a ¼ or ½ section of wheat on the Reservation. I put up one half of the money and you put up the other one half and hire someone to plant it. While you're running around see if you can't run into a piece of ground. I don't think you would have any trouble getting someone to plant it. I think it would be a good investment – because it has to rain up there sometime.

May get laid off soon, or be shipped to some other place. Guess this job doesn't keep you out of the army any more. I have been thinking of the Air Corp if I have to go.

Let me know about that farming.

As Ever,
Dwight

Dear Mr. and Mrs. Alaska:

DON'T FORGET THE SCORE IS NOW 148 JAP PLANES PULLED OUT OF THE SKIES BY OUR FLIERS AND ALLIED FLIERS.

We are frequently asked just what the dues are in the Kayototokyo Club. The score as published in the Anchorage Daily Times last Saturday was 148 planes. That represents the dues for this week — $1.48 — or one penny for every Jap plane pulled out of the skies. What the score will be this week no one knows but whatever the figure is, that figure will represent the dues for next week.

Don't forget to tune in on Radio Station KFQD at 10:15 o'clock, Thursday evening, when we take to the air to tell Alaska about the club, what it has done and what it will do. Try to be at the station when the program goes on, but if you can't, then be sure to tune in. The program will be diversified — not one of those cut-and-dried affairs to which no one cares about listening. There will be music, and chats, and humor, and the things you like to hear.

We now have a theme song — "Kayo-to-tokyo" — which we will introduce Thursday evening. The music and words were written by Jay Smith, local composer with a number of nationally-known song hits to his credit. We like it — and we know you'll like it.

The Anchorage Laundry and Cleaners is the latest entrant into the 100 per cent division. More will be announced this week.

Mrs. Raymer Brown, at J. Vic Brown & Sons, is still at your service. Be sure to call on her for any information you may desire.

It seems as if our dreaming sergeant has stirred up more interest than he imagined with his chance remark that he dreamed of the first plane flown to Alaska with our insignia on the side, a wreath of flowers around the cockpit, the brass band and all of the celebrities and members of the club there to greet it. One lady wanted to know where we were going to get the flowers and another one told her we'd wait until summer and use wild flowers.

All we can say is that regardless of the flowers the plane will be heard round-the-world in no uncertain terms because it is

Newspaper clipping sent back home.

March 4th 1942 #22

Anderson Camp
Anchorage, Alaska
Insert: "War Upset Trapping..."

Dear Folks,

Don't have much to write about but will drop you a line to let you know that I am o.k. and getting along fine.

Most everyone on the base got a raise from 6½ cents to 20 cents per hour. I got 6½ cents but we get time and a half for Sundays. Cat skinners get a dollar seventy per hour and time and one half for Sundays. I may get back on one soon.

Joe E. Brown the movie actor is here visiting the soldiers. He says this town of Anchorage is the largest liquor store that he has ever been in. He is master of ceremonies at the Alaska Golden Gloves Tournament being held here.

I will write again if I can find anything to say.

As Ever,
Dwight

WAR UPSETS TRAPPING ROUTINE FOR SIMCO

Takes Time Out To Watch For Japs While Catching Furs In Wilderness

Home from a five months' Trapping expedition, during which he stood lonely guard among the hills of the Kasina district when news of the Pearl Harbor raid came over the radio, Elmer Simco was back in Anchorage today to spend his "winter vacation."

Simco is one of Alaska's most colorful trappers who has stuck to his trade through depressions and prosperity, shunning high pay defense jobs to patrol his 75 miles of line in the heart of interior Alaska.

This year his vigil was not quite so lonely for Elmer took his bride into the wilderness with him to share the sojourn and take charge of his log home and eight trapline cabins.

Get News Of War

"We heard about the attacks on Pearl Harbor and the Philippines over our battery radio set," Elmer reported today after getting a crop of foot-long whiskers trimmed and tasting for the first time in many months one of his favorite cigars. "I made up my mind no Jap was going to use the Kasina district for a landing field and stood guard with my hunting rifle."

He followed with especial interest the Philippine campaign, he said, because he "soldiered" around Corregidor and Bataan 30 years ago.

Mrs. Simco returned to Anchorage last week and Elmer came in the night before last after a plane picked him up near his cabin and flew him to Talkeetna.

Trapping Good

Trapping was good, he reported, but the work of mushing the trapline was greatly increased by the deepest snow in the district in 12 years. This also drove the caribou away which in turn adversely affected his wolf catch, Simco said.

"Wolves follow the caribou," he explained. "When we went in last September the woods were alive with wolves and we planned on a record catch. But pretty soon it began to snow and the caribou left and so did the wolves."

Their greatest upset of the season was the loss of one of their fine sled dogs.

Wolves Kill Dog

"I left him chained to the cabin while I went out to break trail a little way from the cabin. When I came back, wolves had just about torn him to pieces," Simco related. All of their equipment, including the dogs, were flown in, pound rate, by plane.

The Simcos plan to return to their wilderness home 250 miles from here as usual next year unless Elmer is called to some sort of defense work. He's 55, too old for military service, but he said he was anxious to do anything Uncle Sam would have him do to help win the war.

U. S. Signs Pact With Brazil To U

Newspaper clipping sent back home to his Father, Earl.

March 4 - 42

Dear Folks -

Don't have much to write about but will drop you a line to let you know that I am ok and getting along fine -

Most every one on the base got a raise from 62½¢ to 70¢ per hr. I got 62½¢ but we get time and a half for Sundays. Cost dinners at $1.70 per hr and time and a half Sundays. I may get back on the base soon -

Joe E Brown the movie actor is here visiting the soldiers. He left this town of

will drop you a line to
that I am getting a
we had a bad cold for
couple of da

Mrs Earl

Wallace C. Roberts
1st St

FORT RICHARDSON
MAR 25
2 — PM
1942
ALASKA

3 CENT

VIA AI

March 23rd 1942

Fort Richardson
Anchorage, Alaska

Dear Folks,

Don't have much to write about but I will drop you a line to let you know I am getting along OK. I have had a bad cold for about a week. I didn't work for a couple of days but I am just about over it now.

The censors are getting strict about the mail. We can't send post cards or newspaper clippings. All mail is checked before it leaves the post.

We can't write about the weather now.

I am sending a money order for $20 to pay my lodge dues.

I must go to bed.

As Ever,
Dwight Margrave

P.S. You can send it back.

> "The censors are getting strict about the mail. We can't send post cards or newspaper clippings."

April 14 –

…ar Dad & Mother:

Am still here and getting
…re, was sick for about a w…
have written, had sinnis ha…
a dockter for three days an…
head cleaned out, and took
…ills he gave me and payed …
and am feeling fine now. Ge…
…s but never have receive…
…ot …

FORT RICHARDSON.
APR 18
11 AM
1942
ALASKA

AIR 6 CENTS MAIL
UNITED STATES OF AM…

VIA AIR MA…

April 14th 1942

Fort Richardson
Anchorage, Alaska

Dear Dad and Mother,

I am still here and am getting along fine. I was sick for about a week since I have written. Had sinusitis and I had to go to a doctor for three days and have my head cleaned out. Took a lot of pills he gave me and I paid my bill and I am feeling fine now. I got your letters but I have never received the gloves. I also got Wally's letter. He is pretty well sold on the Navy, it sounds to me like.

I would like to take an examination for a flying cadet. I might be able to make it. I am pretty sure I will be home in July and maybe sooner unless we get stuck up here some way. I am working on a different crew now. I am an asbestos worker; covering steam pipes. It isn't a bad job. I should get on a Cat in about a week or two.

I got a home paper today, and I was glad to see it, although there wasn't anything to read. I only get about one out of every four copies; it seems. I don't know what happens to the rest of them. I bought some tickets on the ice pool. It is a lottery on when the ice breaks up on a river at Nenana. It pays from $50 to $1,000 to the winner. It goes out between the 15th of April and the 15th of May, the one that guesses the minute it goes out wins the money.

A new bunch of men came in and one fellow, Bill Shields of Gordon that I knew was among them. He works for the Air Corps. I was sure glad to see someone that I knew.

Bedtime must close.

Your son,
Dwight Margrave

> *"A new bunch of men came in and one fellow, Bill Shields of Gordon that I knew was among them."*

AS EVER, *Dwight*

Mother's Day card sent to
Dwight's Mother, Pearl - 1942.

ARMY 265th

On August 4th 1942 Dwight E. Margrave enlisted in the 265th Engineer Combat Battalion, within the 65th Infantry Division, and the 869th Ordnance Automotive Maintenance Company.

ORDNANCE CORP

Army 265th Ordnance Company

Ordnance Corp United States Army was founded on May 14th, 1812. It is one of the oldest branches of the United States Army. The duties and responsibilities date back to the colonial era. The broad mission of the Ordnance Corp is to supply Army combat units with weapons and ammunition, including their procurement and maintenance.

The Ordnance Department swelled exponentially in WWII and applied the lessons it learned in WWI. The Ordnance Department was responsible for roughly half of all Army procurement during WWII, $34 billion dollars. President Franklin Delano Roosevelt's 'Arsenal of Democracy' depended on the Ordnance Department to become a reality.

The Ordnance mission in the field operated on a scale never experienced previously by the Ordnance Department. During WWII, the Ordnance Branch gained its third core competency, Bomb Disposal (renamed Explosive Ordnance Disposal after WWII) added to its previous missions of ammunition handling and maintenance. By war's end, there were more than 2,200 Ordnance units of approximately 40 types, ranging in size from squads to regiments. The Ordnance Department applied the maintenance lessons it learned in WWI and devised a five-echelon maintenance system ranging from base shop maintenance to organizational maintenance, all in an effort to return materiel to operational status as near to the front line as possible. To complicate the maintenance mission, in 1942, the responsibility for motor transport was shifted from the Quartermaster Branch to the Ordnance Department. The complexity of maintenance for such a wide variety of vehicles spawned several innovations which continue to the present; a system of preventative maintenance and the publication of Army Motors, renamed PS Magazine in 1951. This maintenance challenge remained one of the largest hurdles in WWII.

AS EVER, *Dwight*

July 28th 1942

Rome Hotel
Omaha, Nebraska

#26

Dear Folks,

Have joined the Army, the 265th Ordnance Company. It is a repair unit. It fixes broken cars and trucks. Leonard and I both signed up in it and I guess we will get to stay together until it is all over.

You do your basic training for about two months and then go to school for about three months and then you are sent somewhere.

I will have to stay here for two or three days and then I will be home for about a month before I am called.

You will find enclosed two forms. Take one to Ross Rosh and the other to Fred Butler and get them fixed up for me. Mail them back tomorrow, Special Delivery. Be sure to send them immediately. If you can't find Rosh take it to Rushville.

As Ever,
Dwight E. Margrave

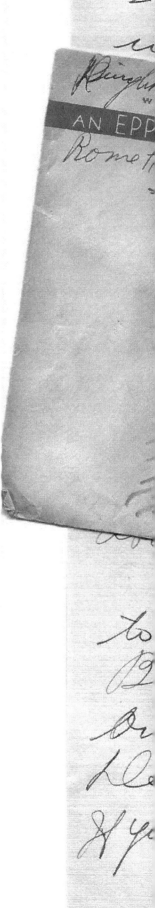

"*I have joined the Army,* **The 265th Ordnance Company.** *It is a repair unit.*"

106

Have joined the Army, the
Ordnance Company. It is a repair
... fixes broken cars and trucks
... signed up in it and
...
...
...

Mr. Earl Morgan
Gordon
Nebraska

JUL 28 7:30 PM 1942 BURLINGTON STA.

d enclosed ... the on
oss Rash and the others to Fred
... and get them fixed up for me
mail them back tomorrow. Specia
ery. Be sure to send them immediately
... and Rash's take it to Rushville
... Ever

Albright E Morgan
Hotel Rome
Omaha

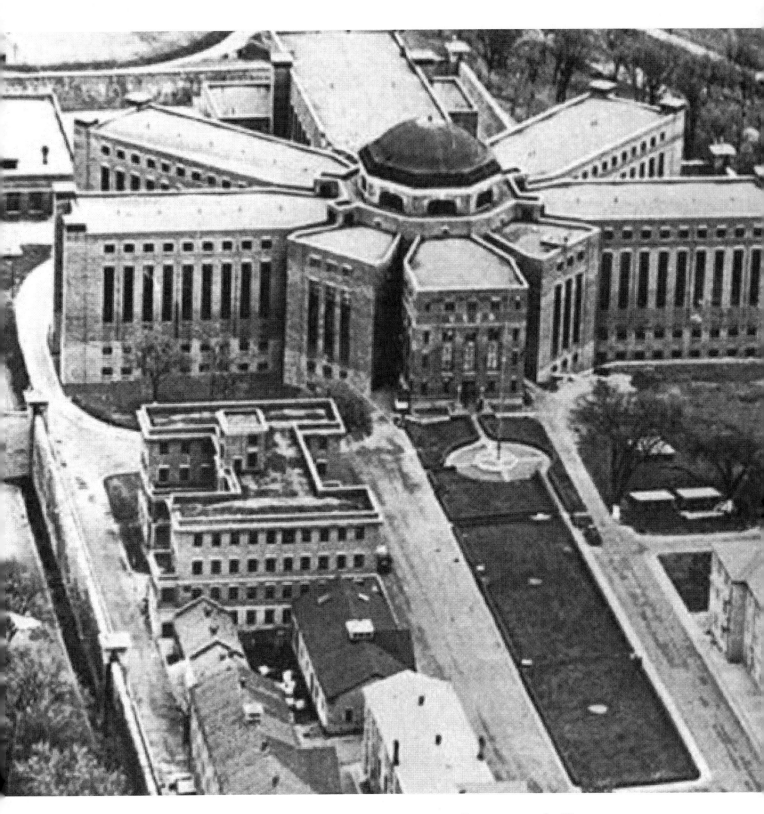

United States Disciplinary Barracks at Fort Leavenworth, Kansas.
(Photo courtesy of the U.S. Army Combined Arms Research Library)

FORT LEAVENWORTH

Circa 1942

Fort Leavenworth was built in 1827. It is the oldest active Army post west of Washington DC, and the oldest permanent settlement in Kansas.

In April of 1942 it became the Army induction center for Army volunteers. The induction station processed 318,000 Soldiers from 1940 to 1946.

The induction process included learning about the four services available. A soldier would go through a physical and mental examination including: hearing test, visual acuity test, teeth examination and blood pressure check. Then have an interview with a psychiatrist. After this the Soldiers were measured, weighed, and examined by surgeons and orthopedist.

Then, accepted or rejected for service.

Dear folks:

Have been getting along. Havent done much of anything but stand in line since I been here. Get up early in mornings and and go to bed early. It is hot as the dickens. A lot worse than it— going on

[envelope:]
AFTER FIVE DAYS RETURN TO
Pfc. ᴅᴇ Margrave
Company D.
Induction Center
Ft. Leavenworth Ka.

Red X Mrs Earl Margrave
Bartley
Gordon
Nebs

FORT LEAVENWORTH
9 AM SEP 20 1942
KANS.

clo—
well
I wish we wants
of here anywhere every

September 18th 1942

Company D, Initiation Center
Ft. Leavenworth, Kansas
Insert: Receipt of issued clothing (next page)

Dear Folks,

Have been getting along fine. I haven't done much of anything but stand in line since I have been here. I get up early in the mornings and go to bed early.

It is hot as the dickens down here; worse than it is in Omaha. There is not much going on or much to write about. The men, draftees and enlisted come in here by the thousands everyday, get their uniforms and get sent out. I have mine now, about all the clothes I can carry. They don't fit very well.

I wish we would get sent out of here, everything was in such a muddle. It couldn't be much worse some place else. It is really one grand mix up here. I saw one of the Bornaman boys and I think he is gone now.

Did you get my clothes?

There is no need to write me here as I will be transferred soon, probably Camp Perry, Ohio.

We are just waiting for shipping orders.

As Ever,
Dwight M.

> "I wish we would get sent out of here, everything was in such a muddle."

RECEPTION CENTER SUPPLY # 1773
Fort Leavenworth, Kansas

ARTICLES OF CLOTHING ISSUED TO TRAINEES

Bag, Barracks	2ea	Gloves, Woolen	1pr
Raincoat	1ea	Cap, Garrison, O.D.	1ea
Shirts, Cotton	2ea	Cap, Garrison, Khaki	1ea
Leggings, Canvas	1pr	Socks, Woolen, Light	3pr
Coat, Working	2ea	Socks, Cotton	3pr
Trousers, Working	2ea	Overcoat, Woolen	1ea
Hat, Working	1ea	Coat, Woolen	1ea
Undershirts, Woolen	2ea	Jacket, Field	1ea
Undershirts, Cotton	3ea	Shirts, Flannel, O.D.	2ea
Drawers, Woolen	2ea	Belt, Waist, Web	1ea
Drawers, Cotton	3ea	Trousers, Woolen	2ea
* TOILET KIT	1ea	Trousers, Cotton	2ea
		Shoes, Service	2pr

*(Contents of this kit shown on reverse side.)
　Equipment shown on reverse side.
　　Initials of Officer witnessing issue of above articles.

Receipt of articles of clothing issued to Dwight at Fort Leavenworth, Kansas - 1942.

my clothes

CONTENTS OF TOILET KIT ISSUED AS SHOWN ON FRONT SIDE OF THIS FORM

Towel, bath	1ea	Razor, safety, w/blades	1ea
Towel, huck	2ea	Brush, tooth	1ea
Handkerchiefs	4ea	Brush, shaving	1ea
Necktie, cotton, khaki	2ea	Comb, rubber	1ea
Necktie, woolen, black	1ea		

EQUIPMENT ISSUED TO TRAINEES

Can, meat	1ea	Canteen	1ea
Knife	1ea	Cup	1ea
Fork	1ea	Cover, canteen	1ea
Spoon	1ea	Soldier's manual, FM21-100	1ea
		Pamphlet, sex hygiene and venereal diseases	1ea

Receipt of articles of toilet kit issued to Dwight at Fort Leavenworth, Kansas - 1942.

September 19th 1942
Reception Center
Fort Leavenworth, Kansas

#28

Dear Folks,

Arrived here yesterday morning and they kept us up until midnight and then up at 4:00am this morning.

I guess we go to Camp Perry, Ohio tomorrow or the next day, as near as we know. We will get uniforms tomorrow, so I will send my clothes home.

As Ever,
Pvt.1st. Class
Dwight Margrave

"SWELL WORK SERGEANT"

AS EVER, *Dwight*

A U.S. Navy training ship at Camp Peary, Virginia, circa 1945. A wooden mock-up of a destroyer escort was built in the fall and winter of 1944 at Camp Peary and used during the 16-week recruit training courses held at the Camp. It was nicknamed "Miss Never Sail" and still stood in 1946. (U.S. Navy).

CAMP PERRY
Circa 1942

Camp Perry is located on the shore of Lake Erie near Port Clinton, Ohio. It was the primary training center for the Ohio National Guard for much of the Twentieth Century.

During WWII Camp Perry became a reception and training center for new Army recruits.

In addition to its regular mission as a military training base, Camp Perry also boasts the largest outdoor rifle range in the world, after the NRA Whittington center.

September 24th 1942

265th Ordnance Co.
Camp Perry, Ohio

#29

Dear Folks,

Just arrived here last night and I had a swell time coming over on the Pullman (Sleeping Car) to Chicago and from there on a special train. I had to do guard duty all the way: two hours on and four off.

I haven't seen much of this camp yet. We drilled most all day and had to move our stuff from one place to another. I had to carry our war bag with all of the clothes in it for about a mile. It weighs about seventy pounds and sure is awkward to carry. Then we went back to get our folding cots and bedding. The bunkhouses don't have lights or showers in yet.

It is certainly cold here. So far, this isn't so bad, only I get tired of standing in line. We put on our wool clothes today.

Love,
Dwight M
Pvt. 1st. Class

"I had to carry our war bag with all of the clothes in it for about a mile."

a swell time coming over
man to Chicago and from
on a special train, I had
guard duty all the wa—

AFTER FIVE DAYS RETURN TO
Pfc. P. E. Margrave
17028445
265 Ord Co
Camp Perry Ohio
2nd letter

CAMP PERRY
SEP 25
8 AM
1942
OHIO

Mrs Earl Margrave
Gordon
Nebraska

the ** supposed to
as stoves in yet and it is
ly cold here. So far this
so bad only I get tired of
in line. Put on our wool
today—
Love Pf [illegible]

Sept 30
Camp Perry

Dear Folks:

Am getting along fine and don't mind the Army so much although the grub isn't very good but they say a sailor that kicks is satisfied.

We get up at 5:20 walk about a half a mile to chow at 6:00, eat out of mess kits, wash them and be out on the drill field at 7:00 Exercise or drill until 11:30, chow at 12:00 usually go to some lecture or drill at 1: until 4:30 chow at 5:00 and then we are usually finished unless we are on a detail or something.

Was on detail this afternoon, had to clean rifles and oil them, they are old Enfields that have been packed in grease since the last war. Some of them look like pretty good guns almost new.

I have a h— of a time marching, I guess my legs are too long any how the rest of the fellows aren't in step with

September 30th 1942

265th Ordnance Co.
Camp Perry, Ohio

Dear Folks,

Am getting along fine and don't mind the Army so much, although the grub isn't very good but they say a soldier that licks is satisfied.

We get up at 5:20am, walk about a half a mile to chow at 6:00am, eat out of mess kits, wash them and be out on the drill field at 7:00am. Then we exercise or drill until 11:30am, chow at 12:00 noon. Then we usually go to some lecture or drill at 1:00pm until 4:30pm. We chow again at 5:00pm and then we are usually finished; unless we are on a detail or something.

I was on detail this afternoon. I had to clean rifles and oil them. They are old Enfields that have been packed in grease since the last war. Some of them look like pretty good guns, almost new.

I have a hell of a time marching. I guess my legs are too long and bow. The rest of the fellows aren't in step with me, but I will get along somehow.

I haven't been off the post yet and don't get to go any place for another week. You kinda get tired of seeing soldiers all the time and no civilians.

Oh, I forgot to tell you, lights out at 9:00pm and it is almost that time. I haven't heard from you. Did you get my grip and the letter I sent? I will write again.

As Ever,
Dwight M.

"I have a hell of a time marching, the rest of the fellows aren't in step with me..."

October 11th 1942

265th Ord. Co.
Camp Perry, Ohio

#31

Dear Folks,

Am getting along fine. They are really training us. We work pretty hard marching and then draw KP or guard duty which kinda breaks the monotony.

We had a big parade here yesterday. Most all of the soldiers on the post were in it and our Company did as well as any of them and we had the least training.

I got to go to town last night, the first time since I have been in. I had a T-bone steak that was only about ½ inch thick. It sure seemed good to eat something besides the army food, even if the steak wasn't very good.

Tomorrow we go out on the rifle range and shoot. They make sure you can get in an uncomfortable position to shoot with a sling wrapped around your arm, but you can hold a gun awful steady that way. I have to stand guard duty tomorrow night.

Send me Marion's address and I will write to her. How is Marge getting along with her school? Let me know what you have heard about Leonard D. One boy in our cabin got a radio today and it has been running all day and I suppose all night.

I must close as it is about bedtime.

As Ever,
Dwight M.

"They make sure you're in an uncomfortable position to shoot with a sling wrapped around your arm."

Camp Perry
Oct 11-42

Dear Folks —

Am getting along fine. They are really training us, work pretty hard marching and then draw K.P. or guard duty which kinda breaks the monotony. Had a big parade here yesterday most all of the soldiers on the post were in it and our company did as well as any of them and had the least training.

AFTER FIVE DAYS RETURN TO
Pvt D. E. Margroes
265 Ord. Co.
Camp Perry Ohio

CAMP P[ERRY]
OCT 12
8 AM
1942

ABERDEEN

Circa 1942

The Ordnance Specialist School for enlisted personnel was transferred from the Raritan Arsenal New Jersey in 1931 to Aberdeen, Maryland.

A separate research division was formed in 1935 and four years later plans were approved for a special building to house a new organization called the Ballistic Research Laboratory Building 328. It was completed in 1941 and provided the facilities to conduct research and experimentation in ballistic and fire control.

By the time the United States went to war in 1941, the need for testing facilities had grown so much that the government was forced to acquire additional acreage for Aberdeen Proving Ground. Seven thousand acres were added in 1942. During the war, personnel grew to peak strength of 27,185 military and 5,479 civilians. All fields of research, development and training expanded and facilities were increased to meet the heavy workload of wartime.

The Research Laboratory was expanded and facilities were increased and achieved increasing prominence in the nations scientific community. The automotive and armor testing activities were greatly enlarged, and the antiaircraft gun testing mission was expanded. A new airfield capable of accommodating the larger aircraft being used for bomb testing was created.

Aberdeen Proving Ground's technological contributions to the war effort include the world's first digital computer: The Electronic Numerical Integrator and Calculator (ENIAC), the first man portable antitank weapons system - (the Bazooka), and the first system-wide practical applications of Statistical Quality control. These statistical theories were developed by Bell Laboratories and were first applied through Ordnance material procurement contracts in World War II.

PROVING GROUND

The explosion of Lester P. Barlow's 'GLMITE' bomb at Aberdeen Proving Ground, Maryland. The 1,000 pound liquid oxygen bomb created a powerful roar, but little damage, 84 test goats near the explosion.

ORDNANCE SCHOOL
ABERDEEN PROVING GROUND
MARYLAND

Aberdeen
Oct 19 - 4[2]

Dear Folks -

We moved over here the 17th
of a job notice to have ev[erything]
being packed including what
[?] supplies we have and ha[ve]
the [?]

Pvt. W. E. Marglow[?]
4-6 5-th Ord Co.
A.P.G.
Aberdeen Md.

Rec'd your let[ter]
after [?]

Mrs Earl Mar[glow]
Gordon
N[eb]

ABERDEEN PROV[ING GROUND]
OCT 2[?]
6 PM
1942
MD

October 19th 1942

Aberdeen Proving Ground
Aberdeen, Maryland
265th Ord. Co.

Dear Folks,

We moved over here the 17th. We got a four hour notice to have everything packed including what equipment and supplies we have and had them on the train. I didn't know where we were going until we were started. I had a good time coming over; only I didn't have but one meal of two sandwiches and coffee in twenty hours.

This is a nice place. They have steam heated barracks and the food has been good. We eat at a mess hall with about one thousand others and they all have Negro help. I never saw so many barracks and soldiers in all of my life, miles and miles of them.

This is a big ordnance training center and also a proving ground where they test tanks, guns and howitzers.

They are sure rushing us through and I think we will be out of here in about a month or six weeks. I don't know where but there are some rumors that we may go to Canada and test new machinery, but I don't believe it.

Our company has been a leading outfit in drill, marksmanship, and had our examinations high average in the IQ test.

I am getting along fine and am feeling okay, although you sure get a work out.

It's time for lights out.

As Ever,
Dwight M.

P.S. 65 miles to Washington D.C. and 125 miles to New York City.

> "*Our company has been a leading outfit in drill, marksmanship and... the IQ test.*"

AS EVER, *Dwight*

October 26th 1942

Aberdeen Proving Ground
Maryland
265th Ord. Co.

#33

Dear Folks,

Am getting along fine and like it here better than Ohio. We have finished our Basic Training and started to school today. They are going to make us a wrecker driver and motor crane operator and might do some test driving of tanks.

The rumor that I told you about in the last letter is correct. We are going north for the winter where there is some very severe cold to test equipment. This is restricted information and so don't spread it around too much or let it get in the papers. We will have a good camp and lots of good clothes but will be practically isolated.

Today I went to school and they sent me with three civilians on a big wrecker truck that sure is a dandy. It has two winch lines; one in front and one in back. It also has a hoist, all power driven by the motor. You can hook a tank on the winch line or on the back of the truck and drag it right along.

Went to New York City Saturday night and stayed over Sunday. I say that is sure a big place. I don't know why so many people want to live so close together.

I saw the sights, the Normandy, the boat that burned. I went up on top of the Empire State Building 1,280 feet high. Rode the subway trains and went under the river in that tunnel. Had a swell time.

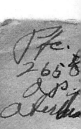

Dad, if you happen to see Bill Reed, get Tom Reed's address from him and send it to me. I think he is in Washington, D.C. and I might get to see him.

As Ever,
Dwight

"We are going north for the winter where there is some very severe cold to test equipment."

ORDNANCE SCHOOL
ABERDEEN PROVING GROUND
MARYLAND

A.P.G.
Oct 26.

Dear Folks —

Am getting along fine and like it here better than Ohio. We have [finished?] our Basic training and started [?] today. They are going to make [?] [?] truck drivers and motor [mechanics?]

[envelope:]
Mrs. Earl Margrave

Gordon

November 18th 1942

Aberdeen Proving Ground
Aberdeen, Maryland
265th Ord. Co.

#34

Dear Folks,

Just have time to let you know that I am alright before I go to breakfast.

I don't have much to write about only that we are leaving soon and will be stationed about 150 miles west of Winnipeg, Canada. We get 20% more money while we are up there, but it will be awful cold to work.

I have a lot of good clothes to wear. Wool and fur, but I will sure need it as the only time we work is when it is 20° below or colder.

I went to Washington D.C., a very beautiful city. I saw Tom Reed and he took me all over town and kept me overnight. His wife is a good cook. It was the first time I got anything good to eat since I have been in the Army.

I will drop you a line before we leave if I can.

As Ever,
Dwight

P.S. My address will be:

PFC Dwight E. Margrave
265th Ord. Co.(MM)
A.P.O. 699
C/O Postmaster
New York, N.Y.

"...the only time we work is when it's 20° below or colder."

**ORDNANCE SCHOOL
ABERDEEN PROVING GROUND
MARYLAND**

Nov 19- 42

Dear Folks-

Just have time to let you know that I am allright before I go to breakfast.

Don't have much to write about only that we —

Rec'd Nov 21

Aberdeen Proving Ground, MD.
NOV 18 6 PM 1942

free

Mrs Earl Margrave
Gordon
Nebraska

Old Camp Shilo
- Joe Schiller Collection, undated.

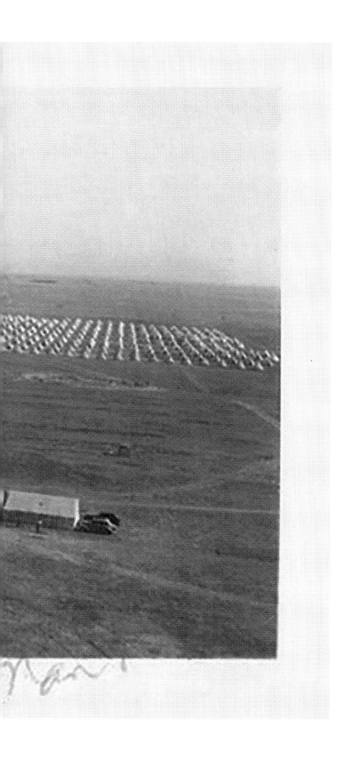

CAMP SHILO

Circa 1942

Camp Shilo is located about 150 miles west of Winnipeg, Canada. During WWII Camp Shilo was home of the A3 Canadian Artillery training. The first Canadian Parachute Battalion arrived at the camp in 1942.

The 265th Ordnance Company was sent to Camp Shilo in the month of December 1942 to test jeeps and other heavy equipment under below freezing temperatures.

ORDNANCE SCHOOL
ABERDEEN PROVING GROUND
MARYLAND

Ft. Lewis - Wash.
Dec 3 - 42

Dear Dad & Mother.

Arrived here about midnite last nite after a very long and uncomfortable train ride, 65 hrs, and only got off of the train two times, about 15 minutes each for exercise. Had trouble on the way, broke a coupling link and lost about half... train was about 4 hrs...

...end -15° bel...

Pfc Dwight Margrave 19078445
268 Ord Co "mm"
A.P.O. 699
% Postmaster
Nt. Nt.

Mrs Earl Margrave
Gordon
Nebraska

December 3rd 1942

265th Ord. Co. (MM)
A.P.O. 699, C/O Postmaster
New York, New York

Camp Shilo, Manitoba

Dear Dad and Mother,

Arrived here about midnight last night after a very long and uncomfortable train ride. It took 60 hours and we only got off of the train two times, about 15 minutes each for exercise.

We had trouble on the way; a coupling link broke and lost about half of the train. It took about four hours getting hooked up in minus 15° degrees below zero and no heat as they had the engine off to get the rest of the train.

Had a Pullman's to sleep in and our own cooks and a mess car. The grub wasn't bad. There were about 400 on the train and some freight of equipment.

We came through Chicago and about one half way across Iowa then turned north thru Minnesota and up to Winnipeg and then over here; about 150 miles west of Winnipeg. It is not over about 500 miles from home if you could go across like the crow flies.

We are under quarantine for a couple of weeks. We can't leave our area. One of the boys that came up here a couple of weeks ago came down with Spinal Meningitis. I guess that is why we are quarantined.

Haven't seen anything to tell you about around here yet, although we have swell barracks and good warm winter clothes issued. We got windproof pants and a coat with wool lining and plenty big. They just have two sizes in the Army, too large or too small.

We had a swell turkey dinner Thanksgiving. Not as good as Mother's but, pretty good. I hope Mom's hen lays as good as they did and you are all feeling fine.

What are you going to do for gas and coffee? They are rationing coffee in the Army now. We are on Canadian's rations until ours get here, not so bad.

As Ever,
Dwight

> "...Spinal Meningitis. I guess that is why we are quarantined."

December 14th 1942

Pfc Dwight Margrave
265th Ord. Co. (MM)
APO 699, C/O Postmaster
New York, New York

Camp Shilo, Manitoba

#36

Dear Dad and Mother,

Just got Dad's letter today and so will sit down and let you know that I am OK. I have had a cold and sore throat ever since we left but am getting over it.

I have been running the crane and now we have a clam shell on it to shovel dirt with, but I don't think I will be on that steady, as I am assigned to automotive and that comes under armor plate.

We went on a convoy trip today about 160 miles. I drove a big truck, a Corbitt, about twice as any in Gordon. It was warm today about 10° degrees above zero, the first warm day we have had.

It is so cold up here my watch froze up and stopped. I went to Winnipeg had a swell T-bone steak, 50¢. The people there sure treat you fine. It is a big town here larger than Omaha.

These Canucks are a fine bunch of fellows. They sure stop and look at some of our equipment. When we get the tanks in then they will have something to look at.

In answer to your questions: We still have the same bunch of men and officers that started out but there has been some more thrown in the company from all over. I don't care about the Gordon Journal as there isn't any thing much in it to read and we have to have heat before we can start the motors.

If I was home I would fix your Ford.

Will close for now,

As Ever,
Dwight

"It is so cold up here my watch froze up and stopped."

ORDNANCE SCHOOL
ABERDEEN PROVING GROUND
MARYLAND

Dec 14-42
9:00

Dad & Mother -

Just got dads letter today and will set down and let you know I am O.K. Have had a bad cold sore throat ever since we left but getting over it.

D.E. Margrave 36984445
55th Ord Co "MM"
APO 699
% Postmaster
N.Y.

and Dec 30

Mrs Earl Margrave
Gordon
Neb

dont have much time to write, am well and getting along O.K.

Wish I was home for Xmas but I guess no one here acts any jurloes —

We get Christmas off unless the think it is necessary to work sure has been cold wose than nebraska —

a little snow —

Merry Christmas

WITH ALL THE GOOD WISHES

that words can express
for a
CHRISTMAS
and a
NEW YEAR
of
real happiness

Dwight

Pfc Dwight Margrave
265th Ord. Co. (MM)
APO 699, C/O Postmaster
New York, New York

Don't have much time to write, I am well and getting along OK.

Wish I was home for Christmas but I guess no one here gets any furloes.

We get Christmas off unless they thinks it is necessary to work, sure has been cold, worse than Nebraska.

We had a litte snow.

Merry Christmas,
Dwight

Christmas card
sent home to Dwight's parents - December 19th, 1942.

December 22nd 1942

Pfc Dwight Margrave
265th Ord. Co. (MM)
APO 699, C/O Postmaster
New York, New York

#38

Camp Shilo, Manitoba

Dear Folks,

Received your letter and Christmas cards. I also got a box of candy from Mary Williams and some of her friends and a letter from the preacher and also a book on religion. Tell Mary thanks for the candy and also the Rev. Stein.

I bet it is tough without any gas, coffee and tires, sugar and etc. You will have to join the Army to get something to eat pretty soon.

We are supposed to get Christmas day off and have a big feed. I would rather be at home and eat some of Mom's Christmas dinner. What is Marge doing for gas while teaching? And is Marion going to be home for Christmas?

We went on convoy yesterday and one again tomorrow. It sure is cold in those trucks driving about 150 miles without any heaters and a cold lunch. We do have very good clothes all but footwear, we only have shoes and overshoes and heavy socks.

I'm not on the crane anymore. It comes under the armor plate division and I am assigned to automotive. So, I am a test driver now. It is a lot of fun to drive those jeeps, but kinda cold with only a windshield, no side curtains.

We have had a pretty heavy snow and it hasn't even thawed on the roof of the buildings since we have been here.

I am wishing all the family a Merry Christmas.

As Ever,
Dwight

*"So, **I am a test driver** now.
It is a lot of fun to drive those jeeps."*

ORDNANCE SCHOOL
ABERDEEN PROVING GROUND
MARYLAND

Camp Shilo
Manitoba
Dec 22 – 42

Dear Folks –

Received your letter and Christmas cards, Also got a box of candy from Mary Williams and some of her friends, A letter from the preacher a

last letter not ans'd

Mrs Earl Musgrave
Gordon
Nebr

rather be at home and eat some of moms christmas dinner. What is Ma

AS EVER, *Dwight*

Model of 'Little Boy'
*the atomic bomb exploded over
Hiroshima, Japan, in World War II.*

DWIGHT EARL MARGRAVE
A SOLDIER'S JOURNEY THROUGH WWII

1943
IT'S GOING TO GET COLD

CANADA'S HOTELS OF DISTINCTION
OWNED AND OPERATED BY
CANADIAN NATIONAL RAILWAY

THE CHARLOTTETOWN, CHARLOTTETOWN
THE NOVA SCOTIAN, HALIFAX
CHATEAU LAURIER, OTTAWA
PRINCE ARTHUR HOTEL, PORT ARTHUR
THE FORT GARRY, WINNIPEG
PRINCE EDWARD HOTEL, BRANDON
THE BESSBOROUGH, SASKATOON
THE MACDONALD, EDMONTON

SUMMER RESORTS
JASPER PARK LODGE, JASPER NATIONAL PARK
MINAKI LODGE, MINAKI, ONT.
PICTOU LODGE, PICTOU, N.S.

WINNIPEG, MAN.   Jan 9-43

Dear Folks:-

Have a week end off so came to Win. the only time we get passes is when the weather is warm. and it got up to a thawing yesterday; the warmest day we had since we have been here.

They work us pretty h[ard]
[...] usual
[...] quit[e]
weather [...]

An[d]
[...]
new cat[...]
I showed [...]

[envelope:]
C.N. 269
CANADIAN NATIONAL
RAILWAYS · STEAMSHIPS · AIRLINES
HOTELS · TELEGRAPHS · EXPRESS

WINNIPEG
JAN 9
4³⁵ PM
1943
MANITOBA

BY AIR MAIL
PAR AVION

Mrs Earl Margout
Gordon
Nebr. U.S.A.

January 9th 1943

The Fort Garry Hotel
Winnipeg, Man.

Dear Folks,

Have a weekend off so I came to Winnipeg. The only time we get passes is when the weather is warm, and it got up to about thawing yesterday. It was the warmest day we have had since we have been here.

They work us pretty hard now. Sunday is usually just another day; we get up at 5:30am and quit at 5:00pm. We have had lots of cold weather and about a foot of snow.

I am still test driving trucks, jeeps and even caterpillar tractors. They shipped in some new Cats and I do the breaking in. I showed one of those Lieutenants how to back a 155mm gun out of the shop with one. He asks how I was going to get that gun out and I told him "just back it out," He didn't seem to think I could so I opened the throttle and really put it out in a hurry. He had his eyes sticking out. It's just like backing one of those scoopers... and I knew I could do it.

Our test course is just like driving over rut runs along a lake in the Sandhills, only it's crooked and lots of trees to dodge. We drive over all of those bumps just as fast as we can go and still stay in the truck. If these stand this course they will stand anything. I drove 78 miles yesterday and would of rather drove 200 in the Sandhills. It wouldn't have been so rough or such hard work. All of the drivers have a sore back most of the time just from the bumps.

Thank you folks for the Christmas presents.

I am feeling fine and I kinda like it up here.

As Ever,
Dwight

> *"I showed one of those Lieutenants how to back a 155mm gun out of the shop with one."*

we may get quarrenteened again [strikethrough]
f the men that were in the same
with him are confined to barrick
now, the other fellow that had that
ot allri[ght] _____ they sent him bac
to the sta_____
I thin___
of some___
stripes.___
___ed a___
___ to go___
I he___
___ n___
are sure good ones.

How does dad get hold of enoug
sugar and coffee to feed all of tho
club wemon?

How much gas do you get a week
Don't have much to

Pfc D L Margrave
265th Ord Co
APO 694 ℅ Postmaster
Ny City

ans'd Jan 24
Rec'd 24

Mrs Earl Margrave
Gordon
Nebraska

U.S. ARMY POST
JA 18 194_ P.M. A.P.

January 19th 1943

Pfc Dwight Margrave
265th Ord. Co. (MM)
APO 699, C/O Postmaster
New York, New York

Camp Shilo, Manitoba

Dear Dad and Mother,

We have been having some cold weather up here. It was minus 41° degrees yesterday morning at 9:00am. We had to get out and start all of the trucks, tanks, and tractors. It was a cold job and took lots of heat. It was cold enough that 10w oil wouldn't pour out of a can that had been outside.

I have been working pretty steady with no Sundays or time off. I am still a test driver, but don't drive much of anything but caterpillars, all kinds. I had to work last night and run the crane. I don't know but I may get put on that on the night shift. I don't want it if I can get out of it, but you do as they say around here.

I heard this morning that another fellow has the spinal meningitis and so we may get quarantined again. Some of the men that were in the same barracks with him are confined to barracks now. The other fellow that had it got alright and they sent him back to the states.

I think that I am up for a rating of some kind, either one or two more stripes. I'll probably get them unless I get mad at some sergeant or lieutenant and tell them to go to the hot place or something.

I bet someone is putting eggs in Mom's chicken nest or those hens sure are good.

How does dad get hold of enough sugar and coffee to feed all of those club women?

How much gas do you get a week?... I don't have much to write about.

As Ever,
Dwight

"I heard this morning that another fellow has the spinal meningitis."

AS EVER, *Dwight*

January 29th 1943

Pfc Dwight Margrave
265th Ord. Co. (MM)
A.P.O. 699, C/O Postmaster
New York, New York

#41

Camp Shilo, Manitoba

Dear Folks,

We have been having some awful cold weather up here, as low as minus 50°, and it hasn't been up to zero this month until yesterday. When it gets 40° or 50° below zero, you just can't get enough clothes on to keep warm for any length of time.

I got a rating the other day, a technician 5th grade. It is the same as a corporal. They put me in charge of the caterpillar tractors that they have up here, about eight or ten of them.

I don't have much to do; that is as far as work is concerned. I don't do much driving, only when they want a tank pulled around or something that is pretty hard to do; then I do it. The other boys up here haven't had so much experience.

We are quarantined and can't leave the camp area, another case of meningitis. One fellow died of pneumonia. There are lots of frozen noses, ears, and a few feet, but not serious. I have frozen my nose a few times but outside of that I have been feeling fine.

Dad, go easy on those soapsuds on your birthday. I wish I was home to help you with a few of them.

They have a new ruling that you can't send packages to soldiers in Foreign Service, so it wouldn't be any use to try to send anything but mail.

As Ever,
Dwight M

*"We are **quarantined and can't leave** the camp."*

ORDNANCE SCHOOL
ABERDEEN PROVING GROUND
MARYLAND

Jan 29-43

Hi folks -

Have been having some awful weather up here, as low as — and hasent been up to zero month untill yesterday when [it was] 40 or 5-0 below, you just can[']t [keep] this[?] on to keep warm

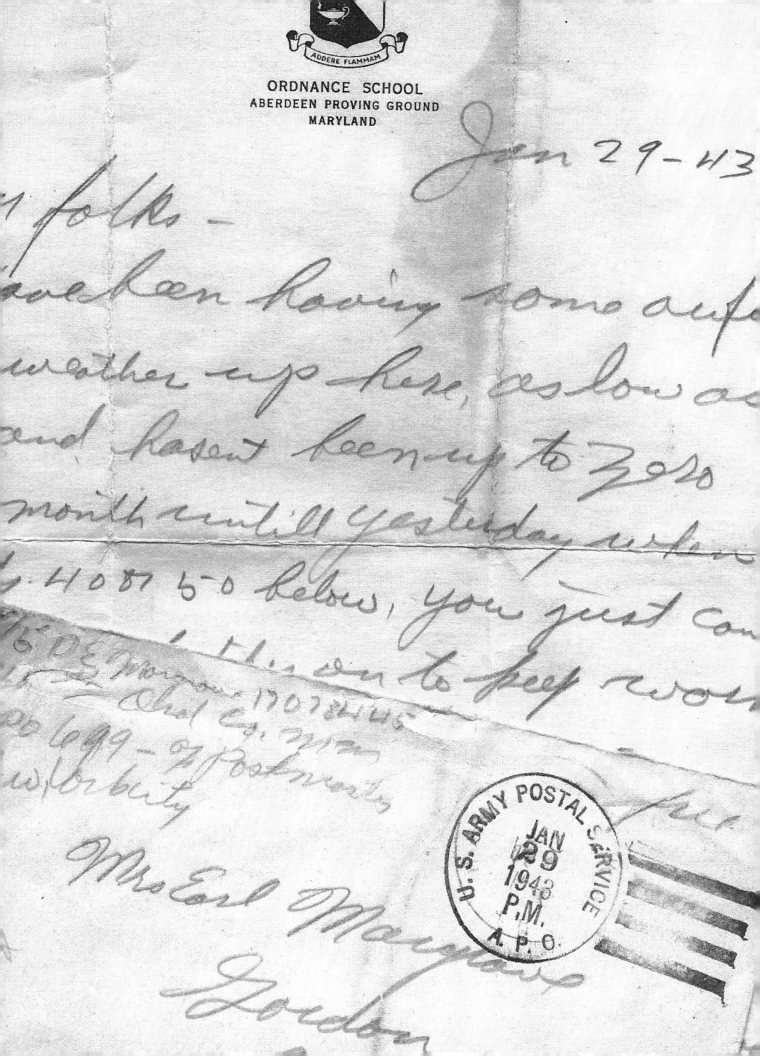

265TH ORDNANCE COMPANY (MM)

Dear Folks,

I don't have much to write but will drop you a line and let you know that I am ok and getting along ok. Haven't did much of any but work for the last few weeks, [off] the other day, and sometimes [we] [work] awhile

T/5 D E Margrave
265th Ord Co (M m) 17098445
APO 699 c/o Postmaster
New York

Miss Earl Margrave
Red Cross

[U.S. ARMY POSTAL SERVICE FEB 16 1943 P.M. A.P.O.]

February 16th 1943

265th Ord. Co. (MM)
A.P.O. 699, C/O Postmaster
New York, New York

Camp Shilo, Winnipeg, Canada

Dear Folks,

Don't have much to write but I will drop you a line and let you know that I am OK and getting along OK. I haven't done much of anything but work for the last few weeks. Sunday is just another day. Sometimes you have to go back and work awhile after supper.

The rumors are that we will be out of here by the 15th of March and go back to Aberdeen. It is hard to tell where from then on, as near as we know; we will probably get a furlough when we get back to the states.

I hope that Marion gets a good job. There should be lots of them now, although I don't know how the field is for her type of work.

I had some excitement last week. I drove a big Cat up on an unloading dock so I could pull a truck off of a flat car.

The dock gave away under the weight of the caterpillar and almost tipped over, but it didn't. It sure tore the dock up, but nobody said anything. We had to tear the rest of the dock down to get out.

We have been issued new rifles. They sure are keen. They are 30 caliber carbine automatics that hold 15 rounds and shoot pretty hard and only weigh four and $\frac{1}{2}$ pounds. It would really make a dandy saddle gun. They are made by Winchester. Just the Ordnance men are the only ones that carry them.

I hope you are all well and feeling fine.

Love,
Dwight

> *"They're 30 caliber carbine automatics... It would make a dandy saddle gun."*

AS EVER, *Dwight*

THE RIFLEMAN'S

Written by Major General William H. Rupertus, *USMC, Retired*

This is my rifle. There are many like it, but this one is mine.

**My rifle is my best friend. It is my life.
I must master it as I must master my life.**

My rifle, without me, is useless. Without my rifle, I am useless. I must fire my rifle true. I must shoot straighter than my enemy who is trying to kill me. I must shoot him before he shoots me. I will...

My rifle and myself know that what counts in this war is not the rounds we fire, the noise of our burst, nor the smoke we make. We know that it is the hits that count. We will hit...

My rifle is human, even as I, because it is my life. Thus, I will learn it as a brother. I will learn its weaknesses, its strength, its parts, its accessories, its sights and its barrel. I will ever guard it against the ravages of weather and damage as I will ever guard my legs, my arms, my eyes and my heart against damage. I will keep my rifle clean and ready. We will become part of each other. We will...

Before God, I swear this creed.
My rifle and myself are the defenders of my country.
We are the masters of our enemy. We are the saviors of my life.

So be it, until victory is America's and there is no enemy, but peace!

CREED -1941

A LETTER GAP

A letter gap from spring 1943 to fall 1943.

There is a time gap or loss of letters. The last letter was dated February 16th, 1943, and in that letter Dwight mentioned that he might have a location move by March 15th and possible furlough after that time.

The next piece of memorabilia is a photograph of Dwight taken by the side of his parent's house in Gordon, Nebraska. On the back of the picture in Pearl Margrave's handwriting is a note and a date of April 1st, 1943.

One can make the assumption that Dwight did indeed receive a furlough and he went back home to Nebraska.

The next letter in the series is dated October 25th, 1943 from "Somewhere in Tennessee" with the envelope postmarked Nashville, Tennessee.

It is possible that Dwight was involved in the construction of the Oak Ridge Tennessee facilities for the Manhattan Project, and this is why there were no letters home.

SPRING/FALL 1943

__Dwight at his parent's home__
in Gordon, Nebraska, April 1st, 1943.

AS EVER, *Dwight*

"SOMEWHERE

Circa 1943

"**Somewhere in Tennessee**" becomes what the US Government called Oak Ridge Tennessee in 1942, the Garrison Headquarters for The Manhattan Project.

The project was created by PRESIDENT FRANKLIN D. ROOSEVELT to research and develop the first atomic bombs.

The job of producing the highly fissionable U235 Uranium isotope, a complicated process, fell to the mysterious top-secret Site X. Several sites were considered but none was as tantalizing as in rural east Tennessee near a sparsely populated spot called Black Oak Ridge.

Near total isolation would keep proceedings secret and prevent the enemy from finding the installation. Cheap hydroelectric power was readily available thanks to the recently completed Tennessee Valley Authority. The settlement grew from 3,500 people to about 75,000 people by 1945.

DWIGHT EARL MARGRAVE
A SOLDIER'S JOURNEY THROUGH WWII

IN TENNESSEE"

Aerial view of the K25 Plant at the Oak Ridge site of the Manhattan Project. This massive building housed the compressors and converters. 1947, photo by Ed Westcott.

Fort Bragg
North Carolina

Tennessee

Dear Folks-

We're still having the rain. Sleeping on the ground and it is getting pretty tiresome. Have had lots of work to do and not much time...

Mrs Earl [Morgan]
[address]
Nashville, Tenn.

NASHVILLE OCT 25 3 PM TENN

May be there two or three of moss — don't know there —

Carl Fuller
Oct-28-43

October 25th 1943

Sgt. D.E. Margrave
265th Ord. Co. MM
APO 402 C/O Postmaster
Nashville, Tennessee

Dear Folks,

We are still here in Tennessee sleeping on the ground and it is getting pretty tiresome. We have had lots of work to do and not much time. We can't have any light on after dark. We can have no fires and it sure gets chilly before morning.

I am still driving the wrecker at present. I am attached to an anti aircraft outfit. We are helping them get their half tracks in shape.

The last time I wrote I had some bad luck. The tent burnt up and all my blankets with it.

Just this last week, I had some bad luck again. I came around a curve with the wrecker pulling a half track and an electric welder. There was a narrow bridge on this curve and the half track went off the bridge but stayed hooked to the wrecker. The welder tore loose and lit in the creek pretty badly broken up. As yet no one has said much about it. It was lucky that no one was hurt. Two men were riding in the half track.

I hope you are all fine and tell the girls to write to me.

How is the pheasant hunting? I would like to help eat some of them.

The food isn't much here.

Your son,
Dwight

"I am attached to an anti-aircraft outfit. We are helping them get their half tracks in shape."

THE MAXWELL HOUSE
NASHVILLE, 3 TENN.

Tennessee's Historic Hotel — The center of the shopping and business district. European Plan.

Sunday

Dear Folks —

Have a two day pass and am in Nashville just taking it easy, eating and sleeping. The first phase of Maneuvers is over and don't think we will have to [...]

Pvt. L. E. Musgrove
5th Ord. Co.
O 402 c/o Postmaster
Nashville, Tennessee

Nashville, Nov 7, 7:30 PM, 1943

BUY WAR SAVINGS BONDS AND STAMPS

November 7th 1943

Sgt. D.E. Margrave
265th Ord. Co. (LM)
A.P.O. 402 C/O Postmaster
Nashville, Tennessee

Dear Folks,

Have a two day pass am in Nashville just taking life easy, eating and sleeping.

The first phase of maneuvers is over and I don't think we will have to stay this winter. Nothing is definite as yet. Our outfit has a record of being one of the best Ordnance Companies in the maneuvers area.

Dad, I saw a bull the other day that I will have to tell you about. Another fellow and I were going down the road in a jeep, and out in a pasture was a white bull that had hair on him about six or eight inches long.

I didn't know about that kind of bull, so we drove up to the house and asked the farmer about what it was. He said that it was a Scottish Highlander bull imported from Scotland. He also had a heifer, the only two in the U.S.

Ask Bob Reed about those long haired cattle. They look like they could stand lots of cold weather.

I don't know where we will go when we leave here, probably Fort Bragg. One of our Lieutenants "Lieutenant Biskeriner" some relative of B.D. is in the hospital in bad shape, rheumatism. We will probably loose him and he is one of our best officers.

I am getting pretty tired of those pup tents. I wake up in the morning and frost is all over every thing and just three blankets per man. Most everyone puts on their overcoats before going to bed. We have even tried blow torches in the tents, but they make to much gas and smoke. Some of the boys have old kerosene lanterns that they use for heat.

I hope everyone is OK. I was glad to hear that Marge and her husband are getting along OK.

Love,
Dwight

"I wake up in the morning and frost is all over every thing."

AS EVER, *Dwight*

November 14th 1943

Sgt. D.E. Margrave
265th Ord. Co. (LM)
A.P.O. 402 C/O Postmaster
Nashville, Tennessee

#45

Dear Folks,

We are leaving here tomorrow for Fort Bragg. We will convoy back about 700 miles and they figure on about two and a half days.

I got to go to town two more days this week. I haven't had much to do. I have been playing football most of the time out here in camps.

It has been awful cold at night. There is frost all over the ground every morning, and sometimes an inch of ice. I will have it lucky going back. My wrecker has a heater in it, the only one in any of the trucks.

I sure will be glad to get out of here, and get back in garrison so that you can wash and sleep on a bunk, most any old bed will seem soft.

I have some good news, we all get furloughs and I will probably get to come home next week. All the boys that go through the maneuvers get a fifteen day furlough. Some of the boys are leaving tonight from here; the rest of us will have to leave from Fort Bragg. Only fifty percent of the company can be gone at one time, and I will be on the last list.

I will write when we get back to Bragg.

As Ever,
Dwight

P.S. My address will be:
Sgt. D.E. Margrave
265th Ord. Co.
Ft. Bragg, N.C.

"All the boys that go through the maneuvers get a fifteen day furlough."

Tennessee Maneuvers

"Somewhere in Tennessee"
Nov. 14 – 43.

Dear Folks –

We are leaving here tomorrow for Fort Bragg, will convoy back about 700 miles and they figure on about 7½ days.

Got to go to town 2 more days this week, haven't had...

[envelope]

Earl Margrave
Hdql Co. 7. T.M.
? % Postmaster
Nashville, Tenn.

Free

NASHVILLE
NOV 16
2:30 PM
1943
TENN.

Mrs. Earl Margrave
Gordon
Nebr.

AS EVER, *Dwight*

FORT BRAGG

Photograph Courtesy of the U.S. Army, XVIII Airborne Corps Archives.

NORTH CAROLINA

Circa 1943

Fort Bragg was founded on the Army's decision to create airborne divisions units of more than 10,000 Soldiers complete with artillery, engineers and support elements in August 1942.

Both the 82nd and the 101st airborne divisions moved to Fort Bragg in the fall of 1942. Fort Bragg served as the airborne training center for these first airborne units.

To augment Fort Bragg, the Army began construction in the spring of 1942 at Camp Hoffman. By early 1943, an airfield was complete along with 1,750 buildings.

November 22nd 1943

Sgt. D.E. Margrave
265th Ord. Co. (LM)
A.P.O. 402 C/O Postmaster
Fort Bragg, N.C.

#46

Dear Folks,

Arrived here last Wednesday and had a good trip coming back. I drove the big wrecker and was in the lead of convoy (30 vehicles). The captain gave me orders to go as fast as possible, which we did. We made a fast trip and no accidents.

I haven't had much to do since we moved in here. It seems good to get into a barracks with beds. But the food isn't so good and you have to start shining your shoes. There is something about living out in the natural world that you like. About half of the boys say that they wish they were still out in the woods.

Half of the men are on furlough now and the other half will get furloughs as soon as they are back, about the 5th or 6th of December.

I will be a little short on money. I would like to borrow about $25 dollars.

One of my buddies wants to come home with me. He lives in California, and doesn't have time to go out there and get back. Would there be any objections if he came along?

I hope everyone is OK and I will be home pretty soon if nothing happens.

As Ever,
Dwight

> "...the food isn't so good **and you have to start shining your shoes.**"

Tennessee Maneuvers

"Somewhere in Tennessee"

Fort Bragg
Sunday

Dear Folks-

Arrived here last week. Had a bad trip coming back. I drove a wrecker and was in the lead of convoy (30 vehickles). The captain's orders to go as fast a possible & we did. Made a fast trip, no accidents.

[envelope postmark: FORT BRAGG, N.C. NOV 22 11:30 AM 1943]

Mrs Earl Morgan

December 31st 1943

Sgt. D.E. Margrave
265th Ord. Co.
Fort Bragg, N.C.

#47

Dear Folks,

Am in charge of Quarters tonight so I have plenty of time to write a letter but not much to write about. I have been doing a lot of drilling and hiking the last few days. My legs are sure sore but I think that they will limber up in a few more days of it, which we will get.

It has been chilly down here. It frosts hard every night or else rains. It is damp and the cold goes right through your clothes.

I will have to tell you about one Sergeant in our outfit. He swears all the time, almost continually. One fellow bet him $5 that he couldn't go all day without swearing. He lasted about 30 minutes and let out a string of curse words. Everyone kidded him about the five-dollar word. This fellow said he would give him a chance to get his money back and he soon had $5 more won. It took about an hour the second time.

I forgot to tell you, I have been going to Jujitsu class, two hours a day. It is sure interesting, but pretty rough stuff. You grab a fellow by the arm and throw him down and all of those trick holds of wrestling. The Lieutenant that teaches it sure can throw you around.

Write.

As Ever,
Dwight

> *"I have been going to Jujitsu class, two hours a day. It is sure interesting, but pretty rough stuff."*

Am on charge of quarters to...
have plenty of time to wr...
letter but not much to wr...
out. Have been doing a lo...
drifting and hiking the la...
days my legs are sure so...
I think that they will lim...
in a few more days of it. w...

E. Morrow
...Co
Bragg N.C.

FAYETTEVILLE
JAN 1
9 30 PM
1944
N.C.

Mrs Earl Morrow
Gordon
Neb

...ted about 30 min...

1944
AWAIT YOUR ORDERS

FORT BRAGG, NORTH CAROLINA

Jan 18 - 44

Dear Dad & Mother:

How have been working pretty hard here lately, lots of train drill and hikes, also lots of

[envelope:]
Sgt. L.E. Margrave
265th Ord Co.
Fort Bragg, N.C.

good letter
3rd letter
arrived

Mrs Earl Margrave
Gordon
Nebr.

[postmark: AGG, N.C. JAN 19 11:30 AM 1944]

because and all of goods good, our hit didn't put the plane down. You don't

January 18th 1944

Sgt. D.E. Margrave
265th Ord. Co. (LM)
Fort Bragg, N.C.

Dear Dad & Mother:

Have been working pretty hard here lately, lots of training drill and hikes, also lots of movie films on army stuff.

I went out on the machine gun range for target practice. I am on a 50 caliber machine gun. I shot at a little remote controlled airplane about 6 feet wingspread and it was from ¼ to ½ mile off and diving and turning. There were five machine guns shooting at it and I got one hit out of 3000 rounds. One hit out of 5000 rounds is good. Our hit didn't put the plane down.

You don't sight these guns, just point them and pull the trigger. Every other round is a tracer and you watch them to see where you are hitting. The gun shoots 800 rounds a minute. The barrels get red hot after about 300 rounds rapid fire. It does not hurt them unless you keep shooting until you melt it. It takes only about two minutes to put in a new one.

We finally got out of this 2nd Army and are attached to the 13th Corp. 6th detachment. I don't know much about it and can't see any change, only we wear a different insignia on our arm in place of the "2".

I have been to the dentist and had one pulled, a wisdom tooth, and four small fillings, and had them cleaned. When you go to these army dentists you don't even get to close your mouth from the time you step in the door until you are finished. I had a pretty good dentist; it didn't hurt much.

I received a box of candy from Sis. It sure was good, but it didn't last long. When someone gets a box of candy around here, everyone stands around until you open it and then dive in.

That is about all I have to write about.

I hope you are all fine.

As Ever
Dwight

> "I went out on the machine gun range for target practice. I am on a 50 caliber machine gun."

P.S. We had about 2 inches of snow the other day. I didn't know if it ever snowed here, but I guess it does.

January 24th 1944

Sgt. D.E. Margrave
265th Ord. Co. (LM)
Ft. Bragg, N.C.

#49

Dear Sis,

That was sure good candy that you sent me and I was glad to get it. You can make about the best candy of anyone I know and I really appreciated it.

What did Glen have to say? Did he think that he would like it in Ireland or not? I suppose that they are still training. It seems like that is all they know to do with soldiers in this damn army is drill and hike.

We were supposed to be pretty "hot" but have cooled off I believe. We are out of the 2nd Army and in the XIII corp. I don't know whether that is better or worse. Anyhow we have started to work again and have quit training as much as we did. We have a lot of trucks and tractors to fix, and some of them are pretty badly shot. I would have lot rather work on tractors than to drill or hike.

I haven't heard from the folks for about a week. In fact I have had only about four letters from them since I was home.

Do you ever see Wilma Spann over in Alliance? I suppose she is still working for the telephone company.

I am getting sleepy. I have been Sargent of the guard since yesterday noon and it is about 6am now. Another two hours and I can go to bed.

As Ever,
Dwight M.

*"What did Glen have to say? Did he think that **he would like it in Ireland** or not?"*

Dear Sis.

That was sure good candy that you sent me and was sure glad to get, you can make about the best candy of any one I know and I really appreciated it.

What did Glen have to say did he think that he would like

[envelope:]
S Margraw
Kent CO
N.C.

FORT BRAGG, N.C.
JAN 24
11 30 AM
1944

free

Mrs Glen Keyser
516 Missouri
Alliance
Nebraska

FORT BRAGG, NORTH CAROLINA

Jan 31 -

Dear Dad & Mother.

Don't have much to write about but will drop you a line to let you know that I am O.K.

Don't know what we are going to do, it seems to be a mystry with

Sgt Lit. Margrave
265th Ord Co
Fort Bragg N.C.

Mrs Earl Margrave

January 31st 1944

Sgt. D.E. Margrave
265th Ord. Co. (LM)
Fort Bragg, N.C.

Dear Dad & Mother,

Don't have much to write about, but will drop you a line to let you know that I am OK.

I don't know what we are going to do. It seems to be a mystery whether we will be shipped out of here, or will stay for the duration. We quit our training drilling and started to work on trucks. We work from 7:30am until 5:00pm, and they seem to be trying to push us pretty hard.

It seems odd, we have to go out in the dirt and sand and there are several big shops on the post that are empty. One has a big electric crane that runs full length of the building and all we have is two tents and nothing in them but tools and oil. It is sandy, just like working in a blowout.

I wish I could be at Dad's birthday party. I hope I can be home for the next one. I have talked to several fellows down here that were stationed at Alliance. Most of them seem to have liked it out there much better than here. They say the civilians treat them swell there.

Happy Birthday Dad.

As Ever
Dwight M.

"We work from 7:30am - 5:00am, and they seem to be trying to push us pretty hard."

February 6th 1944

Sgt. D.E. Margrave
265th Ord. Co. (LM)
Fort Bragg, N.C.

#51

Dear Folks,

Don't know just what to write about, as there isn't much news down here.

We have been having pretty good weather. It rains a little once in a while but has not been a bit of cold, just frosts a little at night. It is a lot different than what you are having.

I was out to the firing range last week for practice with the carbine. I made a fair score. They only give you ten rounds to shoot which isn't enough to hardly get used to your gun. I would like to have some more practice with a 50 caliber machine gun. When you shoot it you really know that you are shooting a gun. It just about deafens you.

They have lots of gliders down here that they pull with planes. I saw a new one sailing around the other day. It is much larger than the plane that pulls it. I don't know just how they get it off of the ground.

I don't know of much more to write about, am OK, and it looks as though we will be here for some time yet.

I hope you are all fine.

As ever
Dwight M.

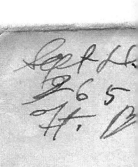

> "*I would like to have **some more** practice with a 50 caliber machine gun.*"

FORT BRAGG, NORTH CAROLINA

Feb 6 - 44

Dear Folks:

Don't know just what to write about, as there isn't much news down here.

Have been having pretty good weather &

Morgraus
Red, CO-
N.C.-

FORT BRAGG, N.C.
FEB 7
6:30 PM
1944

Earl Morgrau
Gordon
Nebr.

February 16th 1944

Sgt. D.E. Margrave
265th Ord. Co. (LM)
Fort Bragg, N.C.

#52

Dear Folks,

Don't have much to write about, but I will let you know that I am OK.

We have been having lots of bad weather down here, rain and sleet. We have to work out doors and it sure has been disagreeable.

I worked all day Monday in the rain and then drew guard duty Monday night and it rained most of the night.

There just isn't much to write about. I haven't been anywhere or had much of anything to do but work on trucks, outside of a four mile run we take every morning. It takes us just 35 minutes to make it. Some of the older fellows can't make it, but so far since I have been in the army I haven't fell out from any march or hike. Maybe that is bragging too much.

You must have had some bad weather at home, from the letter I had of yours. You can always expect that out there.

This is about all for now; hope everybody is OK at home.

As Ever,
Dwight

> *"I haven't been anywhere or had much of anything to do but work on trucks."*

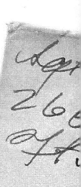

FORT BRAGG, NORTH CAROLINA

Feb 16-43

Dear Folks –

Don't have much to write about but will let you know that I am o.k.

Have been having lots of bad weather down here rain and [...] I have to work out doors [...] agreeable –

AS EVER, *Dwight*

February 23rd 1944

Sgt. D.E. Margrave
265th Ord. Co. (LM)
Fort Bragg, N.C.

#53

Dear Folks:

So you folks are having your winter. Well it seems as though it is all over here. It has been nice and warm the last few days, and no rain. This morning you could run around comfortably in your shirt sleeves even before daylight.

I have been pretty busy and our outfit has lots of work to do changing motors in trucks and general repair work. I have been doing everything from grinding valves to changing motors.

This afternoon they sent me down to help unload a lot of tanks. They were all bolted down to flat cars. All I had to do was to cut the bolts (1 and ½ inches) with the cutting torch.

They are using these tanks to pull the big guns with. A tractor is too slow and not hardly big enough. The big trucks won't pull them: only on the highway, but those old tanks just drag these guns anyplace. The guns weigh about 30 ton.

I was surprised to hear that Marge quit her job. I expect it is lonesome for her over there.

It looks as though we will be here another month or more.

I am sure getting tired of this place.

As Ever,
Dwight M.

> *"They are using these tanks to pull the big guns with."*

P.S. If you see Gealy or any of those guys that have to go to the Army, tell them I said that I would like to get a bunch of those Denver recruits from Gordon to drill. I sure would put blisters on their feet for them —Ha Ha.

FORT BRAGG, NORTH CAROLINA

23/feb/44

Folks:

You folks are having your —, well it seems as though all over here, has been nice

Pvt W.E. Musgrave
5th Ord Co (MM)
Ft. Bragg, N.C.

[postmark: FORT BRAGG, N.C. FEB 24 11:30 AM 1944]

Mrs Earl Musgrave
Gordon
Neb.

everything from grinding to changing motors. This after they sent me down

FORT BRAGG, NORTH CAROLINA

Mar 9-44

Dear Folks-

Dont have much to write about but will drop you a line to let you know that I am O.K. and [...] lots of sleep and

---

Envelope:

Sgt. D. E. Margrave
265th Ord. Co. (M)
Ft. Bragg, N.C.

Postmark: FORT BRAGG, N.C. MAR 10 11:30 AM 1944

Mrs Earl Margrave
Gordon
Nebr.

Rec'd
Mch-12-44

---

send it home some of these [days]
it is absolutely safe so dont [...]

March 9th 1944

Sgt. D.E. Margrave
265th Ord. Co. (LM)
Fort Bragg, N.C.

Dear Folks,

Don't have much to write about, but will drop you a line to let you know that I am OK and getting plenty of sleep and almost enough to eat. (the food has been better here lately) not so much mutton.

We were out on the range today. I fired a Bazooka. It is sure a powerful weapon. I have a dud that has all of the powder taken out of it. I will send it home some of these days. It is absolutely safe; so don't let it frighten you.

What size film does your Kodak take? I can get some 116 or 616 colored films here. If you folks or Marion could use some of it let me know. I will send you a role to try.

I went out yesterday and laid out a map course through the woods. Jack Kronman and I laid it out and the company will have to follow it at night with only a compass. We just stepped it off 100 steps 84° degrees and so on, across creeks, and through thick brush. I bet they have a hard time following it.

I don't have much more to write about. Everybody is talking and hoping for another furlough in another month or two. Hope so.

Hope this finds you all OK.

As Ever,
Dwight

"I fired a Bazooka. It is sure a powerful weapon."

AS EVER, Dwight

March 25th 1944

Sgt. D.E. Margrave
265th Ord. Co. (LM)
Fort Bragg, N.C.

#55

Dear Folks,

Have a lot of news to write about this time, some of it good and some not so good.

We were getting ready to ship overseas and even packing our equipment, when we got word from headquarters of the 13th corps. We would not ship overseas immediately but would be moved from here to some other camp, but it would be in the states. I don't know where but I think it will be maneuvers again in Louisiana. The 13th Corps. Maneuvers begin about the middle of April. I don't know where we will go but Louisiana is my guess.

We had to take physical examinations while getting ready to go overseas. I took mine and I don't think I passed on account of the varicose veins that I have in my leg.

The doctor that examined us said that I should have them cut out and to go to the hospital and have it done. But I don't know whether I want those guys cutting veins out of my leg or not. They don't bother me any but probably will sometime. I don't know just what to do. What do you folks think?

Why don't you folks ask Doc. Vaughn what the results are when they operate and take veins out of your leg, and let me know what he thinks. These army doctors all stick together, right or wrong.

This week we were out on the range to an air show put on by the Air Corps for training to teach you how to identify airplanes and show you what they can do with bombs and machine guns on their planes. They had 30 planes drop about 30 bombs apiece. They also had some dive bombers and ship bombers.

It was a good show but the funny part of it was that these pilots were from about a hundred miles away and didn't know much about the targets they were supposed to bomb. They dove at the bomb proof shelter by mistake and dropped two bombs on it. No one was in it. And another one who was supposed to strike a bunch of dummy trucks they had set up for a target got mixed up and shot holes in some of the trucks that the men came out in. Nobody was hurt.

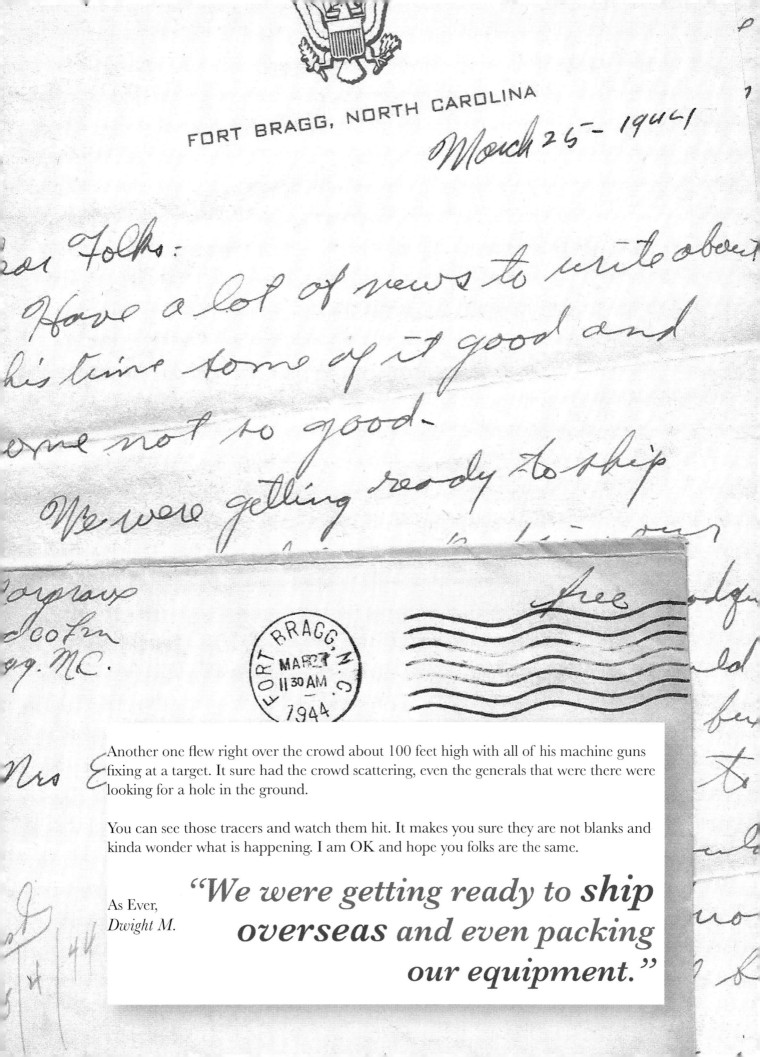

Another one flew right over the crowd about 100 feet high with all of his machine guns fixing at a target. It sure had the crowd scattering, even the generals that were there were looking for a hole in the ground.

You can see those tracers and watch them hit. It makes you sure they are not blanks and kinda wonder what is happening. I am OK and hope you folks are the same.

As Ever,
Dwight M.

"We were getting ready to **ship overseas** and even packing our equipment."

April 9th 1944

Sgt. D.E. Margrave
265th Ord. Co. (LM)
Atlanta, G.A.

#56

Dear Folks:

Expect you will be surprised to hear from me in Atlanta. I happened to get a lucky break and drove a truck down here from Fort Bragg. There were 13 trucks in all. We brought down parts and are loading and taking parts back. I will be back in Bragg Tuesday.

When they send you out in trucks that way, you draw expense money. It amounts to $5 a day to pay your board and room. It sure takes about all that they give you. I am staying at the Y.M.C.A. while here. It is a nice place. I just went swimming a while ago and sure enjoyed it.

I haven't done anything about those varicose veins, but believe I will.

I may get to go to school for about six weeks, nothing definite. Would like to take a welding course.

I am OK and hope you are the same.

Dad, I believe you are having about as much trouble with pink eye as those calves used to have.

Have mom blow sugar in your eyes— Ha.

As Ever,
Dwight

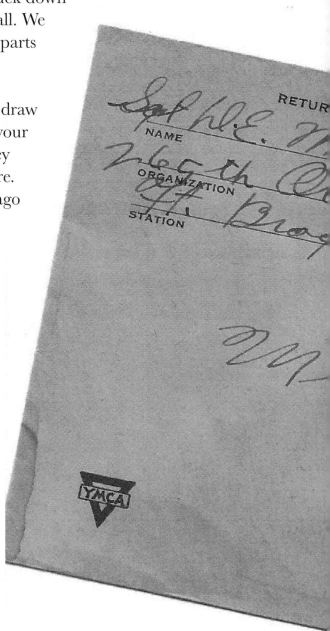

Atlanta [Ga.]
Apr. 9 - 44

Dear Folks:-

Expect you will be surprised to here from me in Atlanta. Happend to get a luckey break and drove a truck down here [...] 13 trucks [...] down [...] and [...] Will [...] Tuesday [...] mountain [...] You can [...] nts to
$5.00 a [...]

Envelope:
ATLANTA APR 10 10:30 AM 1944 GA.
Free
Rec'd 13 - April
ansd.

Earl Margraves
Gordon
Nebraska

Dear Folks:

Arrived back here from Tuesday evening and sure had time. This southern country much good. Poor land and sandy. In all the fields they are planting cotton now one to twenty negroes in ea with a mule hicked he doesn't look

L H Margrave
265th Ord Co. F.M.
Ft Bragg, N.C.

FORT BRAGG, N.C.
APR 14
4 30 PM
1941

free

Mrs Earl Margrave
Gordon
Nebr.

April 14th 1944

Sgt. D.E. Margrave
265th Ord. Co. (LM)
Fort Bragg, N.C.

Dear Folks,

Arrived back here from Georgia Tuesday evening and I sure had a good time. This southern country sure isn't much good, poor land and very sandy. In all the fields you saw they are planting cotton now. From one to twenty Negroes in each field with a mule hitched to a little plow. It doesn't look like they are plowing but more or less just scratching over the top of the ground. It looked like they were plowing then making a row and planting the seed and stringing a row of fertilizer right with the seed. It looks like a slow way to farm.

We are going to get furloughs. Some of the boys are gone now. They are only sending six men a week and my name is pretty far down the list. So I probably won't get mine until the last of June or the first of July.

I don't believe that I will do any thing about those varicose veins until after that time. I also have a chance of going to school in the meantime that I don't want to miss. I may not get to go but I have hopes.

I am in charge of quarters tonight and getting pretty sleepy, but only have a couple of hours to go.

Will write again.

Hope you are all OK.

As Ever,
Dwight M.

"It looks like a slow way to farm."

April 25th 1944

Sgt. D.E. Margrave
265th Ord. Co. (LM)
Ft. Bragg, N. C.

#58

Dear Folks,

Well they changed the furlough list and so the set is now that only seven percent of the company can go at one time and I am 92nd on the list. So, it will be some time before my turn will come.

We are not doing much of anything now; outside of working on trucks and jeeps. Otherwise nothing has happened.

It looks like we will be here all summer or longer, although we might go on maneuvers again, but I don't think so now.

Everyone seems to think that they should send this company home until they decide what they want to do with them.

We have been having good weather, nice and warm and some days are hot.

There has been a lot of rain, but mostly at night. When it rains here it just pours down and then stops; just like someone turning off a water faucet.

I am sending Mom a little trinket to wear. I also have a hand grenade to send along with the rocket. All have had the powder taken out of them so don't let them worry you.

As Ever,
Dwight M.

P.S. It is so damp here the envelopes all stick together before you wet them.

FORT BRAGG, NORTH CAROLINA

4/25/44

Dear Folks

Well they changed the furlow list and so they let now that only 2% of the company can go at one time. Mayraws was on the list

[envelope postmark: FORT BRAGG N.C. APR 25 2:30 PM 1944]

FORT BRAGG, NORTH CAROLINA

May 1-44

Dear Folks:

Won't have much to write about but will drop you a line to let you know that I am —

We are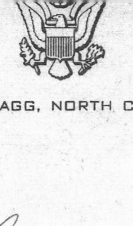
now d...
seem t...
to do...

and there I ...
be about twenty
men that are on detatched
service but all of them
on the post, just out will

Envelope:
Corp E. Margraves
265th Ord. C.O.
Ft. Bragg, N.C.

Mr & Mrs Earl Margraves
Gordon
Nebraska

Field Mays
took 5 do[ys] to
reach here.

May 1st 1944

Sgt. D.E. Margrave
265th Ord. Co. (LM)
Ft. Bragg, N. C.

Dear Folks:

Don't have much to write about but I will drop you a line to let you know that I am OK.

We are not doing much now and I don't know why. We don't seem to have much work to do. It is mostly details here and there. I think there must be about twenty or thirty men that are on detached service but all of them on the post, just out with different companies and so forth.

I have been at the motor pool the last few days. Our motor pool is turning in all of their trucks to another one. They must have had about 500 and it is quite a job to get all the numbers straight and tools and so forth.

Did you get the stuff I sent you? A fellow took the hand grenade home with him on furlough to "Wayne, Nebraska", and was going to mail it from there. I don't know what they would do if the postal inspectors would find it.

We took an eleven mile night hike last week after working all day. I sure had a big blister on my foot. We had to hike with a full pack, rifle and gas mask.

There is a company next door of all recruits with about two weeks in the army. They came from Mississippi. It sure seems funny to see how dumb they are and to think about how dumb we must have been when we came in.

I hope you are all fine and I will write again soon.

I may get to go to Atlanta again in about a week.

As Ever,
Dwight M.

P.S. Thanks for the Bull Durham Hank.

> "*A fellow took the **hand grenade home** with him on furlough...*"

AS EVER, *Dwight*

May 14th 1944

Sgt. D.E. Margrave
265th Ord. Co. (LM)
Fort Bragg, N.C.

#60

Dear Mother and Dad:

Today is Mothers Day; wish I could have been home. It doesn't look like I will get a furlough for another three months yet.

I went to a free show they had the other night, put on by Pepsi Cola Co. It sure was good. They had Strangler Lewis, five times world champion wrestler and about five other wrestlers. They put on a good show. Darren and I went down early and got a ring side seat. One of those wrestlers got thrown out of the ring and lit right on our lap.

One wrestler got the referee and stuck his head in between the ropes. He had him twisted in and then jumped on the ropes. They sure put on a good show. This Lewis is 53 years-old and just as active as a cat. He also gave a talk on wrestling in Japan, India, France and Germany. I guess he was too much for those foreign wrestlers in his time.

I have been working down with the civilian mechanics that rebuild motors and transmissions for trucks here on the post.

I was down there about a week and in the meantime they got in a bunch of prisoners of war, all Germans. They put them to work on trucks and jeeps, some of the older stuff that is used only on the post. They wanted us fellows that were working down there to work with them and show them what to do. I wouldn't go, and told the officers that I was at war with them Nazis— and didn't want to have any thing to do with them unless it would be to shoot them. He said, "That was all right, I feel about the same way." Some of the boys are working with them but don't like it too good.

That is about all I have to write, I hope you are all OK

As Ever,
Dwight M.

P.S. Did you ever get the hand grenade?

FORT BRAGG, NORTH CAROLINA

May 14, 44

Mother & Dad:

[...] is mothers day [...]
I have been home, [...]
like I will get a furlough [...]
other months yet.

[...] to a free show they
[...] other night, put on by
Cola Co. Sure was good

> "I wouldn't go, and told the officers I was at war with them Nazis— and didn't want to have any thing to do with them **unless it would be to shoot them.**"

FORT BRAGG, NORTH CAROLINA
May 31-44

Dear Folks -

Yesterday was Memorial day but just another day here, no parade or speeches. The banks don't even close - seems like that the people down here set the eighth of May as decoration day instead of the 30 -

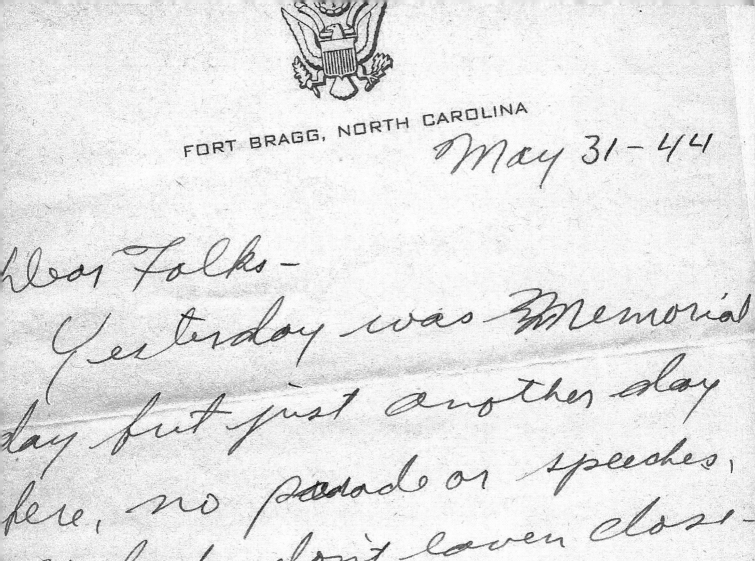

May 31st 1944

Sgt. D.E. Margrave
265th Ord. Co. (LM)
Fort Bragg, N.C.

Dear Folks-

Yesterday was Memorial Day, but just another day here; no parade or speeches. The banks don't even close. It seems like the people down here set the 8th of May as Decoration Day instead of the 30th.

It has sure been hot, not much rain. What little grain they raise around here is ready to cut, and they are still planting cotton and tobacco.

Our company went to White Lake last weekend. It is about 50 miles from here. It is a summer resort on a lake about three miles long and two wide. It sure is a pretty lake, sand bottom and the water is so clear that you can see the bottom of the lake any place. They have lots of cabins, swimming boats and a merry go round to ride on.

We sure had a good time, but some of the boys nearly burned their backs off in the sun. It doesn't take over a half hour in the sun to burn. It seems like it is so much hotter here than it is at home.

I had a chance to go to school but turned it down. It was a general automotive school and I didn't care much for it. I told them that I wanted to go to Diesel Automotive or welding school. They said that there would probably be an opening and I could go.

I am going on sick call this morning to get something for athletes' foot. One foot is sore.

I hope you are all OK.

As Ever,
Dwight M.

> "Our company went to White Lake last weekend. It is about 50 miles from here."

Behind an American flag, a convoy of landing craft head for Utah Beach on June 6, 1944. Each ship has barrage balloon connected by a cable during the D-Day invasion of Normandy on June 6, 1944.

DWIGHT EARL MARGRAVE
A SOLDIER'S JOURNEY THROUGH WWII

JUNE 6th 1944

THE GREAT INVASION

"The great invasion began this morning. We have a radio here and began listening at about 5:30 this morning. I hope Glen made out OK, which from what reports we have heard he probably has."

U.S. Troops land at Normandy on D-Day. With the beach taken and barrage balloons deterring German aircraft, soldiers and supplies flooded into France in June 1944, during World War II.

AS EVER, *Dwight*

Omaha Beach after D-Day. Protected by barrage balloons, ships delivered trucks loaded with supplies. June 7-10, 1944, Normandy, France.

AS EVER, *Dwight*

FORT FISHER

Photo courtesy of John Moseley – Presents Fort Fisher in World War II.

NORTH CAROLINA

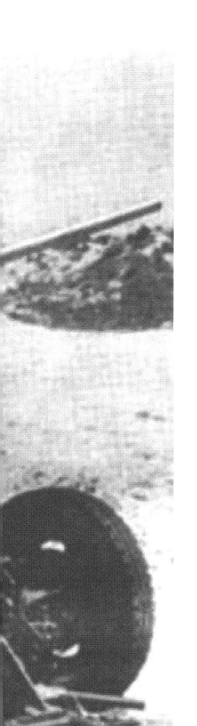

Circa 1944

Headquarters of the 18th Corps School.

Fort Fisher was the site of anti-aircraft training. The operations closed at Fort Fisher in 1944.

Fort Fisher was located south of the main base and became the primary firing range for Camp Davis.

The eighteenth Airborne Corps is a corps of the United States Army that has been in extensive service since WWII. The corps is designated for rapid deployment anywhere in the world and is referred to as "America's Contingency Corps." It's headquartered at Fort Bragg, North Carolina.

AS EVER, *Dwight*

June 6th 1944

#62

Sgt. D.E. Margrave
HQ. 18th Corps School
Ft. Fisher, N.C.

Dear Folks,

The great invasion began this morning. We have a radio here and began listening at about 5:30am this morning. I hope Glen made out O.K., which from what reports we have heard he probably has.

I moved down here Sunday on detached service. There are four of us out of our company here: two mechanics and two small arms men. This fort is about twenty miles south of Wilmington, North Carolina and built right on an Island. The Atlantic Ocean is about two hundred yards to the east and Cape Fear to the west.

About all they do down here is train gunners "anti aircraft." They shot a quarter million rounds in three days here last week. They have planes towing targets for the machine gunners to shoot at and also have rockets that are about six feet long and travel at about five hundred miles per hour. The gunners shoot at them to get an idea how fast some of these planes fly. They also shoot all sizes of anti aircraft guns at targets and sleeves towed by planes.

This other fellow and I work on the trucks that they use here to transport men and guns.

This is sure a nice place; cool all the time with a breeze off of the ocean. There are lots of pine trees for shade and lots of sand. It is worse than blow out in the sandhills, real loose white sand. It sure makes those old army trucks grunt to get around, but they get around pretty good.

There are miles of white sandy beach where we can go swimming every night. I was going to go last night but I went down to the beach and the water was too rough. There were waves that were eight foot high rolling in. It didn't look too good to me.

There is a big summer resort five miles up the beach. We haven't been there, but will go up some evening. I hope you are all OK.

As Ever,
Dwight M.

P.S. Write to me at HQ 18th Corps School, Fort Fisher, North Carolina as I will be down here for two or three weeks.

FORT BRAGG, NORTH CAROLINA

Pfc Fisher
June 6-44

Dear Folks-

The great invasion began this morning we have a radio here and began listening at about 530 this morning

[envelope:]
E. Marqlaus
[?] Corps School
Fisher N.C.

WILMINGTON
JUN 7
1 PM
1944
N.C.

Free

Mrs Earl Marqlaus
Gordon
Nebraska

FORT BRAGG, NORTH CAROLINA

Ft. Fisher
June 12-44

Dear Folks -

Tomorrow I will be 2[?]
years old, seem like tha[t]
getting pretty old but [I]
guess not. Have been h[ere]
down here a[...]
swell [...]
this [...]
like [...]
how [...]

[envelope:]
Cpl. W. E. Margrave
HQ 13th Corps [...]
Ft. Fisher N[C]

Mrs Earl M[...]

[postmark: WILMINGTON N.C. JUN 13 PM 1944]

June 12th 1944

Sgt. D.E. Margrave
HQ 18th Corps School
Ft. Fisher, N.C.

Dear Folks,

Tomorrow I will be 28 years old. It seems like that is getting pretty old, but I guess not.

I have been having a swell time down here at this camp. It is just about like a vacation, I hardly have any work to do. I get up at seven in the morning and have an hour and a half at noon and quit at 4:30pm.

I went fishing yesterday morning. I caught some fish but they were all small; nothing to brag about.

I went swimming yesterday in the afternoon. I had lots of fun playing in those waves that come rolling in. The only trouble with swimming in the ocean is that you will be standing in water about chest deep one minute and the next minute it will be about four feet over your head. If you swim when those waves come in you can just ride over the top of them. It sure is fun.

One of the fellows got a letter today from a fellow in the company at Ft. Bragg. He said that our captain had been shipped to the P.O.E. and they were breaking the company up and sending the men to different companies.

It's hard to tell, I may be transferred some where else if this is so. We plan on going to Fort Bragg this weekend and finding out what is taking place.

I hope you folks are all OK.

As Ever,
Dwight M.

> *"Tomorrow I will be 28 years old. It seems like that is old, but I guess not."*

Fort Bragg
June 27—

Dear Folks—

They pulled us fellows ba[ck]
from Ft. Bragg fishes to Ft.
Bragg again so I don't know for
sure what is going on here no[w]
The rumors are that the com[pany]
ill be split up, only keep 23 in
[the company] to train new men
[and the others] are being [sent]
[somewhere, I'll] get to [...]
[...] doesn[...]

[envelope:]
Pvt. D E Musgrove
765th Mil Co
Ft. Bragg N.C.

Mrs Earl Musgrove
Gordon
Nebr.

FORT BRAGG N.C.
JUN 23
12 — M
1944

June 22nd 1944

Sgt. D.E. Margrave
265th Ord. Co.
Ft. Bragg, N.C.

Dear Folks,

They pulled us fellows back from Ft. Fisher to Ft. Bragg again so I don't know for sure what is going on here now.

The rumors are that the company will be split up and only keep 23 men for a cadre to train new men. Even the officers are being transferred.

I don't think I will get to stay with the cadre but it doesn't make much difference I guess. I would hate to have to teach all of those fellows basic training any how.

I don't have the least idea where we will be transferred to but probably will stay in Ft. Bragg or else some of these other camps here in the south.

Mom, I got your package the other day. It sure was good candy. Thank you and Marge. I have been on guard duty all night and just have an hour to go yet. I am using the hood of a jeep for my writing table this morning. Every time I tried to go to sleep last night a mosquito would bite me.

Our Captain was "Shanghaied" out of the company and sent overseas, no one knows why.

Dad, this company splitting up will probably stop the furlough for a while, and here I was just thinking about writing and telling you to kill a yearling that I would be home before long. But I don't know now. It may be a little bit too soon.

As Ever,
Dwight

P.S. My address is still 265th Ord., Fort Bragg, as far as I know.

> "Our Captain was 'Shanghaied' out of the company and sent overseas, no one knows why."

Ft. Bro
July 2

Dear Folks-

Am being shipped tomo
Camp Rucker Alabama
wenty of us out of this
going down there in to a
pany. It is the 937 Or[d]

Sgt. W.E. Margrave
65 Ord. Co.
Ft. Bragg N.C.

July 2nd 1944

Sgt. D.E. Margrave
265th Ord. Co.
Fort Bragg, N.C.

Dear Folks,

Am being shipped tomorrow to Camp Rucker Alabama. Seventy of us out of this company are going down there into another company. It is the 937th Ord. I think, but do not know for sure. We have heard that it is a heavy auto maintenance. If it is I should be all right.

I have not heard whether this is a new company just being formed or just what. I will write and let you know my address and all about it as soon as we arrive there.

I went to Camp Picket, Virginia last week. I drove some truck up from here and came back on the train. I got up there fine but had a very miserable trip coming back. We had to wait on trains and after we got on one we had to stand up with no sleep the night before.

That is about all for now. I will have to start packing.

I hope you folks are all O.K.

As Ever,
Dwight M.

"It is the **937th Ord**...We have heard that it is a **heavy auto maintenance**."

AS EVER, *Dwight*

CAMP RUCKER

Headquarters at Camp Rucker, Alabama, circa 1940
Courtesy of the U.S. Army Aviation Museum.

ALABAMA

Circa 1944

Camp Rucker, Alabama was later called Fort Rucker. The post provided training for the US Army infantry combat troops headed for service overseas.

The post was the primary flight training instillation for U.S. Army Aviators.

Camp Rucker was also used to train dozens of units of less than division size. These included tank, infantry replacement and the Women's Army Corps as well as specialized units.

During the later part of WWII several hundreds of Germans and a few Italian prisoners of war were housed on the southern edge of the post.

Dear Folks:

This sure is about t[he worst]
camp of all that I h[ave been]
in. It is hot, no plac[e to sleep]
...isn't very g[ood]

Sgt. L.E. Morgrave 17038445
93? Ord (H&M)
Camp Rucker Alabama

CAMP RUCKER, ALA.
JUL 11 2:30 PM 1944

Mrs Earl Morgrav[e]
Gordon
Nebraska

very long
us that have
up with all this

July 10th 1944

Sgt. D.E. Margrave
937th Ord. (HAM)
Camp Rucker, Alabama

Dear Folks,

This sure is about the worst camp of all that I have been in. It is hot, no place to go, the food isn't very good and they sure do work you. I had to work until 9:30pm two nights last week, and also Sunday.

Most of the fellows in this company haven't been in the army very long and so those of us that have been have to put up with all this basic training stuff again, which is pretty tough.

I went outside of the post this evening and had a big steak. It was sure good, but cost $2, pretty high, but a $1 steak is only about four bites.

It must be about time for haying to be in full swing. I bet that Boy Hands are probably scarce. They have fellows in this outfit that couldn't cut grass with a corn knife after a years training. Sure some terrible misfits.

I will get along somehow even if I don't like it here.

As Ever,
Dwight M.

> "They have fellows in this outfit that couldn't cut grass with a corn knife after a years training."

UNITED STATES ARMY

Camp Ruck[er]

Dear Mother & Dad "Grandp[a]

Well I was glad and little excited about being a uncle, would like to see baby,

Things are not so good

[envelope:]
S/Sgt R.E. Musgrove 17078445
937 Ord (HAM)
Camp Rucker
Alabama

Mrs Earl Marg[rove]
Gordon
Nebraska

CAMP RUCKER, ALA. JUL 18 2:30 PM 1944

July 18th 1944

Sgt. D.E. Margrave
937th Ord. (HAM)
Camp Rucker, Alabama

Dear Mother and Dad "Grandparents,"

Well, I was glad and a little excited about being an uncle. I would like to see the baby.

Things are not so good down here, but I guess there are soldiers in places that are a lot worse than this, and probably working harder, but I still don't like it here.

I have been working in the shop as a mechanic here doing every thing from putting in rings, inserts, to motors. We have a nice shop to work in but the tools they have are not so good. We had better tools in the 265th.

Some of the fellows got a good break. Fifteen were sent to school in Ft. Crook, Nebraska for twelve weeks. All but one out of our original company most of them live in eastern Nebraska or Kansas.

May get to go with the next group that leaves. I am sure trying to get to go, they are sending more.

That is about all for now.

Hope you are all OK.

As Ever,
Dwight M.

> "*Some of the fellows got a good break. Fifteen were sent to school in* **Fort Crook, Nebraska** *for twelve weeks.*"

UNITED STATES ARMY

July
Camp

Dear Folks,

Sure hated to hear
Eben, too bad, seemed li[ke a]
nice fellow. Makes it
for sis, and tho [perhaps]
there is nothing for he[r to]
do but brace up and

to mor[row]

Cpl. H E Margrave 17078445
737 Ord Co.
Camp Rucker, Alabama.

[Postmark: CAMP RUCKER, ALA. JUL 31 5:30PM 1944]

Mrs Earl M[argrave]

DWIGHT EARL MARGRAVE
A SOLDIER'S JOURNEY THROUGH WWII

#68

July 31st 1944

Sgt. D.E. Margrave
937th Ord. Co.
Camp Rucker, Alabama

Dear Folks,

Sure hated to hear about Glen, too bad. He seemed like a nice fellow. It makes it bad for sis, and the baby but there is nothing for her to do but brace up and go ahead.

I get to leave tomorrow on furlough. It will probably take about three days to get home from here. The railroad and buses are terrible slow down here. I can make pretty good time when I get as far as Nashville, Tennessee.

That is about all for now.

See you the last of the week.

As Ever,
Dwight M.

> "I sure hated to **hear about Glen,** It makes it bad for sis, and the baby."

GLEN KEYSER

Dwight's sister Marjorie Margrave and Glen Keyser, 1943.

1921 - 1944

Dwight's sister, Marjorie Margrave met her first husband Glen Keyser when he was stationed at the Alliance Air Base in Alliance Nebraska. They met in 1943.

Glen was born on June 16th, 1921 in Beadle County, South Dakota. He had two brothers, Lloyd and Buck along with three sisters. They lived in Wessington Springs, South Dakota.

Glenn died on June 23rd, 1944 after the Normandy Invasion. Aunt Marge was nine months pregnant at the time of his death. She says one of the deepest regrets of her life is she didn't have his body brought back from France. He is buried in The Normandy American Cemetery and Memorial.

Marge gave birth to their daughter Carol Ann Keyser on July 7th, 1944. Carol Ann was born with a mental retardation and a speech impediment.

Aunt Marge married her husband's brother Lloyd Keyser in 1948. They had five children, one baby girl was still born. They were married for 37 years until Lloyd's death in 1985. He was 65 years-old.

Lloyd was drafted for military services in 1942. He belonged to the 145th artillery unit serving in the South Pacific. He was honorably discharged in 1945 after participating in five invasions including Tinian, Saipan and Okinawa. He was awarded the Distinguished Unit Badge, the Philippine Liberation Ribbon with one star, and the Good Conduct Medal.

August 20th 1944

Sgt. D.E. Margrave
937th Ord. Co.
Camp Rucker, Alabama

#69

Dear Folks,

Arrived back to camp OK, although I was pretty tired when I got here.

I got to Omaha with Stienhouse. About 9:00am the next morning I left for Chicago. That night I caught a streamliner. It was sure a good one as it just took eight hours from Omaha to Chicago. The train had an air conditioner, nice soft chairs and a radio in every car. It is sure a swell train, better than the Burlington, and much better than the one that runs from Chicago on down here.

I sure had lots of good eats with you folks. It seems a lot different down here. We had stew the first meal here.

How is the baby, still cries at night and sleeps all day? I bet she will probably get over that after while.

I am going to a ball game this afternoon, so I better get ready.

You folks talk about how hot it was at home, you should see it down here. It's a lot worse.

As Ever,
Dwight M.

> *"That night I caught a streamliner. It was sure a good one as **it just took eight hours** from Omaha to Chicago."*

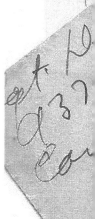

August 31st 1944

Sgt. D.E. Margrave
937th Ord. Co.
Camp Rucker, Alabama

#70

Dear Hank:

Guess it is about time I drop you a line and let you know that I am OK. I am Sargent of the guard tonight so not much to do but write letters.

Sorry to hear of Fred's death. He was sure a good fellow and had lots of fun in his lifetime. Katherine probably is pretty much broken up.

I heard that your Mexican saddle was pretty much of a flop. I thought that it sounded too good to be true, but as long as you broke even it is OK.

I just happened to think, your birthday was August 29th. Greetings! Better late than never.

I am sending a money order for $30. Keep twenty and give Sis ten, and I will send some more next month.

Hank, I got a break. I get to go to Fort Crook to school for eight weeks. It starts Sept. 23rd. It is an engine refurbishing school, which should be all right.

That's all for now.

As Ever,
Dwight

P.S. One thing, when you write send me Leonard's address and also Chet Abrams, if you can find out what it is.

> *"Sorry to hear of Fred's death. He was sure a good fellow and had lots of fun in his lifetime."*

Camp
31 ai[...]

Hank:
Guess it is about [time I drop?]
you a line let you [know]
I am O.K. Am [on?]
guard to nite so [don't have?]
[time?] but write letters [...]
[sorry?] to hear of [...]

Sept 7 - '44
Camp Rucker

Dear Folks:

Got to go to school in Ft. Cook Nebr. Begins the 23 of this month will leave here about the 20th.

Sure looks like Germany will be knocked out in a short while, but acording to the paper won't have much chance of getting out for some time.

Have a big shop to work in and have 4 rookies working under me. Trying to teach them to be mechanics, but

September 7th 1944

Sgt. D.E. Margrave
937th Ord. Co.
Camp Rucker, Alabama

Dear Folks,

Get to go to school in Ft. Crook, Nebraska. It begins the 23rd of the month. I will leave here about the 20th.

It sure looks like Germany will be knocked out in a short while, but according to the paper we won't have much chance of getting out for some time.

We have a big shop to work. I have four rookies working under me. I am trying to teach them to be mechanics, but I don't believe they will amount to much. I have been working hard and lots of nights. I had last weekend off so I went to Panama City, Florida and had a good swim. It was a nice place down there, but very expensive. It cost the two of us $10 for a hotel room for one night.

Well I have to go to work soon. I have worked all day and I have to work from 8:00am to 11:00pm tonight.

Sorry to hear of Fred Duerfeldt's death. He was sure a fine old man.

That's all for now.

As Ever,
Dwight

> "It sure looks like **Germany will be knocked out** in a short while."

AS EVER, *Dwight*

FORT CROOK

*1944 - B-20 shown at Fort Crook, Nebraska. The Enola Gay was a modified B-29.
Courtesy of National Photo Archives.*

NEBRASKA

Circa 1944

More than a year before the Japanese attacked Pearl Harbor, the 17th infantry was pulled from Fort Crook, and it became a maintenance and supply depot and induction center. Dwight first signed up for the army in Omaha, Nebraska, his home state.

During WWII, the federal government requested to build two new aircraft factories at least 200 miles from the center of the United States. The site of the new plants would be south of Omaha at Fort Crook.

Peter Kiewit & Sons became the primary contractor on the 15 million dollar project which would include three runways, a primary structure covering 1.2 million square feet, and 41 smaller buildings, adding another 800,000 square feet. What would become normal wartime precision.

(The last B-29 was produced there on September 18th 1945. The plant closed the following April, becoming a warehouse for Air Material Command. Part of the old fort became a work camp for Italian prisoners of war.)

Oct 10—
Ft Crook

Dear Folks:

Have been pretty busy a[ll]
keep you going from 5:30
in the evening and usu[ally]
ve to study a while at nig[ht]
[other]s, I have been getting go[od]
it is a good course that I [am taking]
instructors seem to know w[hat]
are doing. The one that [I have]
about 60 and has been a[n instructor]

October 10th 1944

Sgt. D.E. Margrave
Co. B.O.A.S.
Ft. Crook, Neb.

Dear Folks,

Have been pretty busy down here. They keep you going from 5:30am until 5:30pm in the evening and I usually have to study a while at night. So far I have been getting good grades and it is a good course that I am taking. The instructors seem to know what that they are doing. The one that I have is about sixty-years-old and has been a mechanic all of his life.

Wrote to the C.O. for a delay in route when the school is finished and I think I will get to be home for a few days after finishing school.

Received my voting ballot today and will fill it out and send it. I don't think that I will make an X in front of Franklin D.

We don't get passes, only from 6:00pm Saturday night, until 11:00pm Sunday. I intend to go out and see the Kothernans some Sunday.

This would sure be a good place to be stationed permanently. These permanent personnel around here don't know what being in the Army is, as far as that goes the ones that run the school don't either, but it is a good school.

How is the corn crop on the farm? Did it get hard or is it soft corn? We had the first frost here last night.

I will write again and let you know if I have to do extra duty because my grades are not up to passing.

As Ever,
Dwight M.

> *"I received my voting ballot... I don't think that I will make an X in front of Franklin D."*

October 20th 1944

Sgt. D.E. Margrave
Co. B.O.A.S.
Ft. Crook, Neb.

#73

Dear Folks,

Last time I wrote I told you that I had sent for a delay in route when school here is finished. The answer came back today, No— so there is no way that I can get to come home.

I have made the highest grade in the course that I am taking for the last two weeks. I get my picture in the Ft. Crook paper and there will also be a copy sent to you folks and to the Gordon paper. You should get yours about the first of next week.

I don't have much to write about, as all you get done here is go to school, tear down engines and rebuild them.

I like the course and like it here. I wish I could stay longer, but I have only two more weekends here. I wish I could get home but it is impossible.

That is about all for now.

As Ever,
Dwight

"I have made *the highest grade in the course* that I am taking."

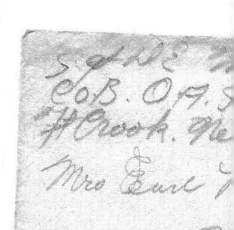

20/10/44
Ft. Crook

Dear Folks:

Last time I wrote I told you that I had sent for a delay in route when school here is finished, the answer came back today, No - so there is no way that I can get to come home.

Have made the highest grade in the course that

October 24th 1944

Sgt. D.E. Margrave
Co. B.O.A.S.
Ft. Crook, Neb.

#74

Dear Sis,

Received your box of candy a couple of days ago and it was so good that I horded it and just finished it a while ago. It was too good to give away Thanks sis.

Sis, why don't you come down next weekend, catch the train Friday night and you would be here Saturday morning. Let Mom take care of Carol Ann. It would do you good to get away from home a few days and I would like to have you come so I could see some of the family while I am so close to home. I won't get a chance to get home, as they will not give me any time off.

I have a girl friend down here. She is very nice and lives in Iowa. She teaches school here in Omaha.

If you can come send me a wire where to meet you as this will be my last weekend here.

As Ever,
Dwight

> "Sis, why don't *you come down next weekend*..."

24/10/44.

ED • FORCES • OF • THE • UNITED • STATES

Dear Sis:

Received your box of candy couple a days ago and was so good that I hid and just finished it while o. It was too good to give way. thanks Sis.

Sis, why don't you come own next catch the

17078445

FORT CROOK OCT 25 5 PM 1944 NEBR.

d you

ing, let

Glen Kayser

o arm

e B

November 12th 1944

Sgt. D.E. Margrave
937th Ord. Co.
Camp Rucker, Alabama

#75

Dear Folks,

Arrived here Friday night after a tiresome trip. That pheasant was sure good that mom fixed for me to take on the train. I wish I had of had enough of it to last all the way to Alabama.

Sure was nice to be home with you folks although it was an awful short visit.

There are a lot of rumors that we will move out of this camp before very long. I hope that is right, as it probably will not be a much worse place; unless it is in the South Pacific or some place like that.

It will probably be some other camp here in the south if we move at all.

I don't have much to write about, hope that you are all well and that the baby won't keep you up too much.

As Ever,
Dwight

Dwight and his Mother while stationed at Fort Crook, Nebraska.

[return address, partially visible:]
...back to...
...H. Rucker Ala.

Camp Rucker —
12/Nov/44

Folks —

Arrived here Friday after a tiresome [trip?]. That Phenobarb was good that [morn?] for me to take the train, wish I [?] had enough to last all the [way] to Alabama. Sure was nice to [be] home with you [folks] although it was an awfull short visit. There are a lot of rumors that we will move out of camp before very [long,] hope that we [do] as it [isn't] a [nice?] place, [it's un-] [like] the So. Pac[ific] place like t[his] probably [some] [where] in the [south,] move at all, have much t[o] [?], hope th[is finds you] all well a[nd] baby [isn't] up too [much].

As Ever
Dwight —

AS EVER, *Dwight*

November 22nd 1944

Sgt. D.E. Margrave
937th Ord. Co.
Camp Rucker, Alabama

#76

Dear Folks,

Tomorrow is Thanksgiving Day. We are to have a big turkey feed and all the trimmings. It will be a good feed but not like as if Mom cooked it.

We have to work all day and as far as that goes we have been pretty busy ever since I have been back from school. We worked until 2:30am last night. All of the ordinance companies on this post have been shipped overseas and that leaves us all the work to take care of.

I made another rating the other day. It gives me one more stripe and will pay a little more money.

There are several rumors that we will go overseas in about two months, but I have my doubts about it.

I haven't had a letter from any of you since I have been here. I have been wondering what the matter is.

I wish I could be home and help you eat Thanksgiving Dinner.

As Ever,
Dwight

Dear Folks

Tomorrow is thanksgiving
& we are to have a big turk
feed and all the trimmings,
will be a good feed but not
like as if mom cooked it.
We have to work all day
& as far as that goes we have
been pretty busy ever since I
have been back from school.
worked untill 2:30 last nite

17078445

five [illegible] company
shipped
all the

CAMP RUCKER ALA. NOV 23 2:30 PM 1944

got here Sunday Gr.

Margrave

ARMED · FORCES · OF · THE · UNITED · STATES

Camp Rucker
Dec 13 - 44

Dear Hank -

Haven't written for some time, last week I had to work three nites untill 2:00 A.M. and inbetween times I spent most of my time in low flown on the bunk.

Had a tough day today and am C.Q. tonite so will try to get a letter written and a few cards mailed.

Had a physical fitness test today, first we had to do 34 pushups, 2nd, 300 yd dash 3rd body a soldier 75 yds on your back in 20 sec.,

December 13th 1944

Sgt. D.E. Margrave
937th Ord. Co.
Camp Rucker, Alabama

Dear Hank,

Haven't written for some time. Last week I had to work three nights until 2:00am and in between times I spent most of my time in low down on the bunk.

I had a tough day today and I am C.O. tonight so I will try to get a letter written nd a few cards mailed.

I had a physical fitness test today. First we had to do 34 push-ups.

Secondly, we had to do a 300-yard dash.

Third, we had to carry a soldier 75 yards on our back in 20 seconds.

Fourth, we had to do 11 burpies in 20 seconds.

Fifth, we had to do 50 yards half running and half crawling in 30 seconds, and last we had to hike four miles with pack and rifle in 50 minutes.

So I feel as if I had put in a good days work today.

Guess we are not going to Mississippi for a while according to the latest rumors.

Hank, did you hear of the WAC whose slip showed and she was discharged from the Army?

As Ever,
Dwight

*"Guess we are **not going to** Mississippi for a while."*

CAMP SHELBY

56th ST. AND 2nd AVE., CAMP SHELBY. This is the business avenue of the camp. Most of the regimental Post Exchanges and regimental recreation buildings face this street.

MISSISSIPPI

Circa 1944

Since 1917, Camp Shelby has served as a training site for various military branches. The camp exceeded the troop capacity of 100,000 in 1944.

Over 17,000 workers and Army engineer units were employed in the construction of Camp Shelby and 1,000 new buildings were raised up.

Camp Shelby's area expanded into the Desoto National Forest, containing 360,000 acres and with an additional 400,000 acres used for maneuvers space, totaling over 1,000 square miles used for infantry training.

At this time the camp hosted the 37th and the 38th infantry divisions for training, also the quarters for the 442nd Regimental Combat Team.

During this time a prison camp for German prisoners of war camp was also added.

Dec 25 – 44
Camp Shelby M[iss]

Dear Folks –
 Moved in here last Saturday and don't think that I will like the camp very well. Although it has been very nice and warm the last two days. We were out playing ball this afternoon just in undershirts.
 Did you get the packages that I sent home, couldn't find any to send. Sgt W.E. Margrave 12078445
937 Ord. Co.
Camp Shelby Miss
Chewin
the fun

December 25th 1944

Sgt. D.E. Margrave
937th Ord. Co.
Camp Shelby, Miss.

Dear Folks,

Moved in here last Saturday and I don't think that I will like the camp very well, although it has been very nice and warm the last two days here. We were out playing ball this afternoon just in undershirts.

Did you get the packages that I sent home? I couldn't find much to send but cigars for Dad and chewing gum for the rest of the family. I also sent some pecans, which I hope you will all enjoy eating. We had a good Christmas dinner. I am sending you a copy of the menu.

We go out in the field tomorrow for three weeks. I hope it doesn't rain too much or get cold, because there isn't much shelter living in a pup tent.

This is a large camp and just built out of tar paper shacks. Some of them are five men huts and others hold about fifteen, but there are thousands of them strung out about five miles.

It sure was good candy that Sis sent. We enjoyed it very much.
I will write and let you know about life in the field in Mississippi.

As Ever,
Dwight

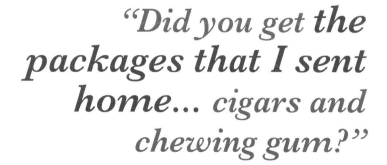

"Did you get **the packages that I sent home**... *cigars and chewing gum?*"

Dec 31 - 4[?]
Camp Sh[...]

Dear Folks:-

Just received your pac[kage]
a few days ago and so I [...]
have to try out this pen, seem[s to]
write pretty good.

Thank you for the Christmas [box,]
all of the presents and that
cake was sure good, smels [like]
it had some brandy in it [but]
was not as strong as the min[ce]
pie that Geo. Hagland alway[s talks]
about.

We are out in the field l[iving]
in tents and sleeping on the g[round]
Sure had seven days wet rain[y we]

December 31st 1944

Sgt. D.E. Margrave
937th Ord. Co.
Camp Shelby, Miss.

Dear Folks,

Just received your package a few days ago and so I will have to try out this pen. It seems to write pretty good.

Thank you for the Christmas box and all of the presents. That first cake was sure good; smelt like it had some brandy in it, but not as strong as the mince pie that George Hayland always told about.

We are put in the field living in tents and sleeping on the ground. We have had several wet rainy days and are not allowed to build fires to dry out by. When it isn't raining it is very nice and warm; only the mosquitoes have been bad.

The company drew for four free tickets with the expenses paid to the Sugar Bowl game in New Orleans tomorrow. I wasn't lucky enough to draw one. I sure would have liked to go.

Well about two more weeks in the woods and we will get to go back in to our little tar paper shacks in the camps.

You folks were good guessers as to what I wanted for Christmas, and sent just what I needed, thanks again.

I will write again soon. Ben Durrer went home on furlough for Christmas, his first since he was home with me.

As Ever,
Dwight

> "We are put in the field *living in tents and sleeping* on the ground."

1945
THE PACIFIC THEATER

*Battleship USS Pennsylvania is followed by cruisers.
They enter the Lingayen Gulf to support the U.S. Invasion of Luzon Island.
January 1945. Philippines, Pacific Ocean, World War II.*

January 18th 1945

Sgt. D.E. Margrave
937th Ord. Co.
Camp Shelby, Miss.

#80

Dear Folks,

Haven't written for some time but I didn't have much to write as we have just moved in out of the field for the first time since the day after Christmas. We worked all the time and had quite a bit of rain. We had breakfast and supper in the dark and were not allowed to have any lights, so you see it was pretty hard to get a chance to write.

I have some good news. I will get a furlough next month and so don't be surprised if I come walking in some time during the first of February.

I am in charge of quarters tonight so I have to stay up all night and post guards, answer the telephone, and wake the men up in the morning.

Not much news here; only that it seems good to get off of this cold wet ground and get to sleep in the barracks.

That's about all for now. I will write and let you know when I will get this furlough.

As Ever
Dwight

> "I have **some** good *news.*"

ARMED · FORCES · OF · THE · UNITED · STATES

Camp Shelby
Jan 18-1-45

Dear Folks-

Haven't written for some time but didn't have much chance to write as we have just moved in out of the field for the first since the day of his ~~Marg~~ worked all

Marg ave 12078445
d. H. A.M. Co-
Shelby Miss.

Mrs Earl Morgans
Gordon
Nebr

ARMED · FORCES · OF · THE · UNITED ·

18, Feb-

Dear Folks-

Arrived here last nite, late and had a good trip coming down here. It was and raining in K.C. and but out down here it

T/3 W. E. Margrave 17078445
937th Ord. H.A.M. Co.
Camp Shelby Miss.

Mrs Earl Ma
Gordon

February 18th 1945

937 th Ord. HAM. Co
Camp Shelby, Miss.

Dear Folks,

Arrived here last night. I wasn't late and had a good trip coming down here. It was snowing and raining in Kansas City and St. Louis, but down here it is nice and warm, We hardly need a fire in the shacks we live in.

I sure had a good time while I was home and I really enjoyed the good food and everything. It makes this army life easier to get to go home once in a while.

How is Dad's card bunch getting along, good I hope.

I had to fill out cards of change of address, which will be sent as soon as we leave. We will probably finish packing equipment this week. We will have to work about every night until 11:00pm. We are supposed to go from here to the P.O.E. in Seattle Wash, as near as we know about the 15th of next month.

Hard to tell where this outfit will end up at. We might go to Alaska. You can't be sure of anything until you arrive.

That is all for now,

I will write again.

As Ever,
Dwight M.

> "How is Dad's card bunch getting along, good I hope."

AS EVER, *Dwight*

THE WEDDING

Mr. Dwight E. Margrave

ANNOUNCEMENT

Ms. Irean Jacobson

AS EVER, *Dwight*

#82

WESTERN UNION
A. N. WILLIAMS, PRESIDENT

CLASS OF SERVICE
This is a full-rate Telegram or Cablegram unless its deferred character is indicated by a suitable symbol above or preceding the address.

SYMBOLS
DL=Day Letter
NL=Night Letter
LC=Deferred Cable
NLT=Cable Night Letter
Ship Radiogram

The filing time shown in the date line on telegrams and day letters is STANDARD TIME at point of origin. Time of receipt is STANDARD TIME at point of destination

3WM X NL PD

HATTIESBURG MISS MAR 25 1945

MR MRS EARL MARGRAVE

GORDON NEB

MISS IREAN JACOBSON AND I WERE VERY HAPPILY MARRIED LAST NIGHT BY A CHAPLAIN ON THE POST DAD COULD YOU WIRE ME $50 THIS GETTING MARRIED IS RATHER EXPENSIVE BUT THINK I WILL LIKE IT VERY MUCH

SGT D E MARGRAVE

804A

THE COMPANY WILL APPRECIATE SUGGESTIONS FROM ITS PATRONS CONCERNING ITS SERVICE

1945

THE GORDO[N]

Jacobson-Margrave

On Saturday, March 24, at the Post Chapel at Camp Shelby, Mississippi, Miss Irean Jacobson, daughter of Mr. and Mrs. Henry Jacobson, and T/3 Dwight E. Margrave, son of Mr. and Mrs. Earl Margrave, were married by the Chaplain in the presence of few of the groom's Army friends.

After a honeymoon in New Orleans the groom left for a Port of Embarcation on the west coast. Mrs. Margrave after a visit with a brother at Anton, South Carolina, will return to Denver where she is a window stylist for a department store.

Both Mr. and Mrs. Margrave are former students of the Nebraska State Teachers' College. Mr. Margrave is a graduate of the Gordon High Schools and pior to entering the Army was employed in construction work in Alaska. Mrs. Margrave graduated from the Chadron Prep High School.

ABSOLUTELY FIREPROOF

Forrest Hotel
150 ROOMS   150 BATHS
RATES FROM $2.00
CIRCULATING ICED WATER AND CERTIFIED LIGHTING
IN EACH GUEST ROOM
ALL ROOMS AIR COOLED

Hattiesburg, Miss.

MAX M. MABEL
MANAGER

Married the 24th of March

25/Mar/45

Dear Folks.

Expect that you were surprised to hear that I am married, well I surprised my self but

Just go[t]

is pro[...]

as any[...]

I th[ink]

sure [...]

We w[...]

I have which will next to

[envelope:] Forrest Hotel — 150 ROOMS 150 BATHS — B.C. YOUNG MANAGER — Hattiesburg, Miss.

HATTIESBURG MISS. MAR 26 4 30 PM 1945

Mrs Earl M[...]
Gordo[n]
Neb[...]

March 25th 1945

Forrest Hotel
Hattiesburg, Miss.
Sgt. D.E. Margrave
937th Ord. Co.
Camp Shelby, Miss.

Dear Folks,

Expect that you were surprised to hear that I am married. Well I surprised my self but just got to thinking that now is probably just as good a time as any.

Irean is a very nice girl. I think a lot of her and am sure that you folks will. We will live here until I leave which will be next week. Then she will go to Denver and live with her sister. Here is a little more about her. She is a window decorator. She fixes up windows in these large department stores, which I guess is a pretty good job.

About the money you sent. I have made out an allotment to Mother that is $50 a month. So Mom can pay Dad back out of that money. It will continue as long as I am in the army. Use it if you need it. Irean will also get $50 a month and that will leave about $34 for me when I get overseas which will be plenty.

Don't know where we will be sent but I expect it will be either the Philippines or China.

I may be in Seattle for a few days; if so I will get to see Spann.

Hope that you folks don't think that I am foolish for getting married as I am happy and want you to feel the same.

I have had three, three day passes this month and will get one more, not bad.

Love,
Dwight

"*I expect that you were surprised to hear that I am married.*"

March 30th 1945

Forrest Hotel
Hattiesburg, Miss.
Sgt. D.E. Margrave
937th Ord. Co.
Camp Shelby, Miss.

#84

Dwight and his bride, Irean, before shipping off to the Pacific.

Dear Folks,

Enjoying married life very much. If I had realized that it's this nice I would have probably been married years ago. Irean is really a swell girl and I am sure that you will like her.

We will be shipped to the P.O.E. next week. I will go to Seattle.

I have had lots of time off in fact I haven't been in camp only long enough to get another pass in the last two weeks.

I will have to go back to camp tomorrow. There will be a big parade then we will have Sunday off. Irean says we will have to go to church (Easter Sunday) and then I will be restricted Monday morning until we leave here.

Will write again soon.

As Ever,
Dwight

*"Enjoying married life very much. If I had realized **that it's this nice** I would have probably been married years ago."*

MAX M. MABEL
MANAGER

Forrest Hotel

150 ROOMS 150 BATHS
RATES FROM $2.00
CIRCULATING ICED WATER AND CERTIFIED LIGHTING
IN EACH GUEST ROOM
ALL ROOMS AIR COOLED

Hattiesburg, Miss.

Mar 30 - 45

Dear Folks -

Mrs Earl Margrove
Gordon
Nebraska

like her -

```
CLASS OF SERVICE

This is a full-rate
Telegram or Cable-
gram unless its de-
ferred character is in-
dicated by a suitable
symbol above or pre-
ceding the address.
```

The filing time shown in the date line on telegrams and day letters is STANDA[RD]

3WM X NL PD

HATTIESBURG MISS APR 1

EARL MARGRAVE

GORDON NEB

DAD CAN YOU LOAN ME 50 MORE. IF P[OSSIBLE SEND]
IT AT ONCE AM LEAVING IN THE NEXT [FEW DAYS]

SGT D E MARGRAVE

750A

#85

1201

SYMBOLS

DL = Day Letter

NL = Night Letter

LC = Deferred Cable

NLT = Cable Night Letter

Ship Radiogram

at point of origin. Time of receipt is STANDARD TIME at point of destination

LE WIRE

AYS

Dear Folks: At Sea

Om on a boat somewhere in the
ocean and not enjoying the trip too
much. It is not like it was when
I went to Alaska, going up there you
could see land most of the way here you
can't see anything but water.

This is a pretty good ship but
very crowded and the food is terrible
the mess hall smells like a garbage
can but you have to eat anyhow.
Haven't been sea sick yet, some
of the fe[llows]
may co[...]
a bit m[...]
water.

[envelope:]
T/3 Dwight E Margrave 17098445
937 Ord. (HAM) Co.
A.P.O. 18636 c/o Postmaster
San Francisco Calif.

APR 23 1945 POSTAL SERVICE
Rec'd Sept 28 - April 1945

Mrs Earl Margrave
Gordon Barnes
Nebr.

PASSED BY 49972 S EXAMINER

We left [...]
got to [...]
so. Ha[...]
got to [...]
you where. Had a long trip
across the o[cean]

April 25th 1945

Dwight E. Margrave
937th Ord (HAM) Co.
APO 18636 C/O Postmaster
San Francisco, Calif.

At Sea

Dear Folks,

Am on a boat somewhere in the ocean and not enjoying the trip too much. It is not like it was when I went to Alaska. Going up there you could see land most of the way. Here you can't see anything but water.

This is a pretty good ship but very crowded and the food is terrible. The mess hall smells like a garbage can but you have to eat anyhow. I haven't been seasick yet. Some of the fellows have but my turn may come. I guess we have quite a bit more time to spend on the water.

I haven't had any mail since we left Mississippi. I don't know if Irean got to Denver OK or not but expect so. I had some time off at the port. I got to go on pass but can't tell you where. I had a long trip across the USA to the port. There was lots of snow in the mountains.

I don't have anything to do on this ship only pull four hours of guard a day, but that just helps use up the time, so I don't mind it much.

Write as I will get your letters eventually and I will be glad to hear from you. I don't know when this will be mailed but soon I hope.

As Ever,
Dwight

> "The mess hall smells like a garbage can but you have to eat anyhow."

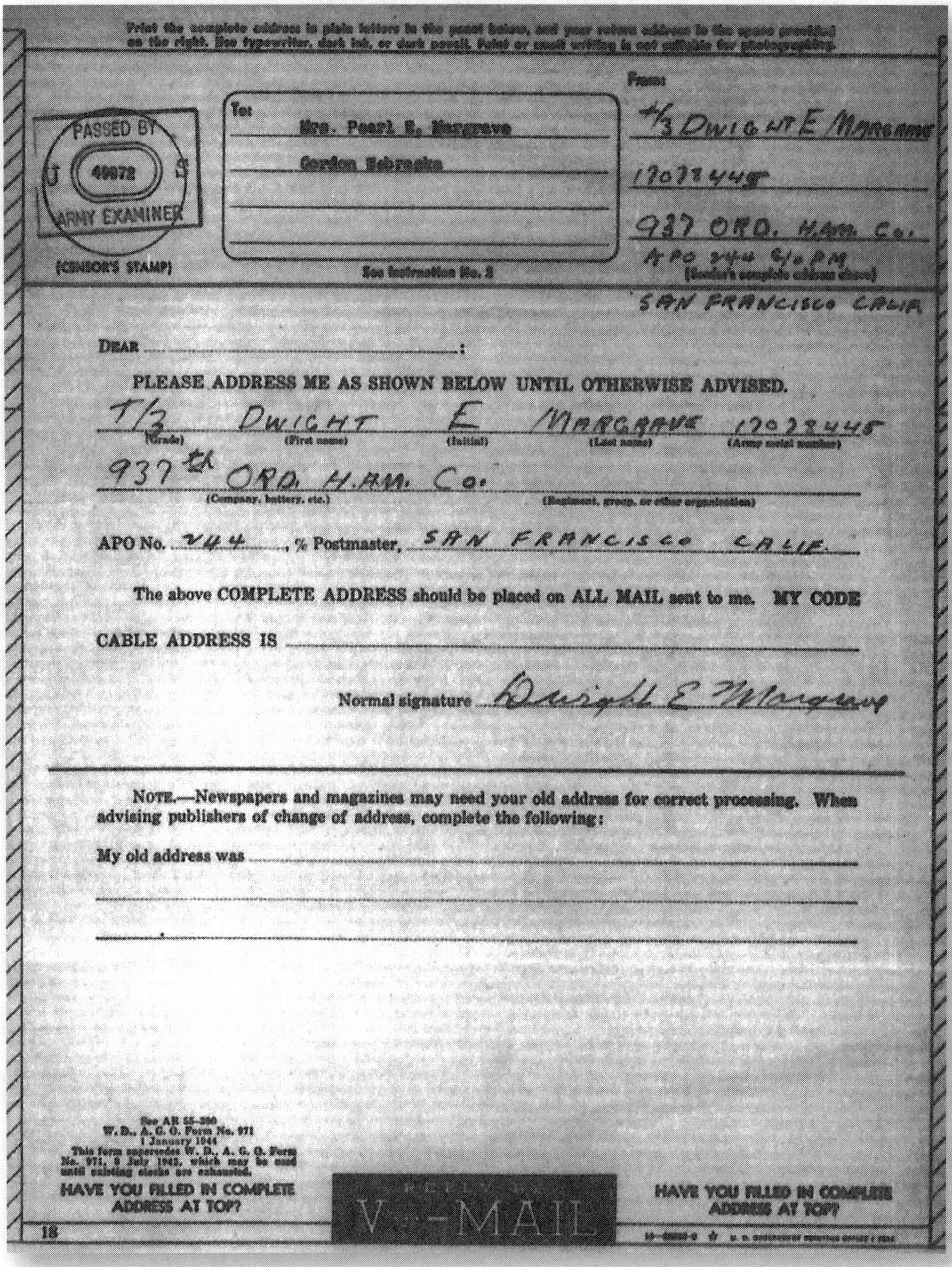

Print the complete address in plain letters in the panel below, and your return address in the space provided on the right. Use typewriter, dark ink, or dark pencil. Faint or small writing is not suitable for photographing.

To:
Mrs. Pearl E. Margrave
Gordon Nebraska

PASSED BY
U 49872 S
ARMY EXAMINER
(CENSOR'S STAMP)

See Instruction No. 2

From:
T/3 DWIGHT E MARGRAVE
17028445
937 ORD. H.AM. Co.
APO 244 c/o PM
(Sender's complete address above)
SAN FRANCISCO CALIF

DEAR ....:

PLEASE ADDRESS ME AS SHOWN BELOW UNTIL OTHERWISE ADVISED.

T/3 (Grade) DWIGHT (First name) E (Initial) MARGRAVE (Last name) 17028445 (Army serial number)

937th ORD. H.AM. Co. (Company, battery, etc.) (Regiment, group, or other organization)

APO No. 244, % Postmaster, SAN FRANCISCO CALIF.

The above COMPLETE ADDRESS should be placed on ALL MAIL sent to me. MY CODE CABLE ADDRESS IS ....

Normal signature Dwight E Margrave

NOTE.—Newspapers and magazines may need your old address for correct processing. When advising publishers of change of address, complete the following:

My old address was ....

See AR 55-380
W.D., A.G.O. Form No. 971
1 January 1944
This form supersedes W. D., A. G. O. Form No. 971, 8 July 1943, which may be used until existing stocks are exhausted.

HAVE YOU FILLED IN COMPLETE ADDRESS AT TOP?

REPLY BY V—MAIL

HAVE YOU FILLED IN COMPLETE ADDRESS AT TOP?

18

#87

DWIGHT EARL MARGRAVE
A SOLDIER'S JOURNEY THROUGH WWII

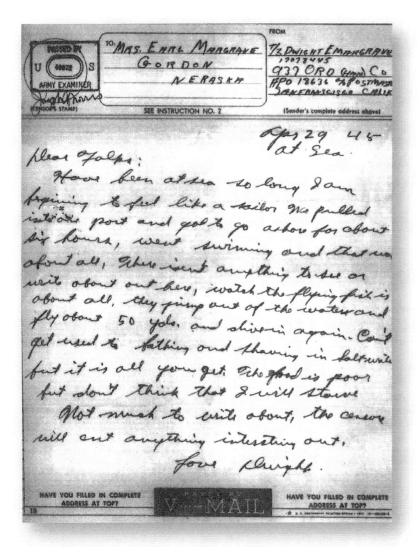

Dwight E. Margrave
937th Ord (HAM) Co.
APO 18636 C/O Postmaster
San Francisco, Calif.

Dear Folks:

Have been at sea so long I am beginning to feel like a sailor. We pulled into our port and go to go ashore for about six hours, went swimming and that was about all. There isn't anything to see or write about out here. Watch the flying fish is about all. They jump out of the water and fly about 50 yards, then swim again. Can't get used to bathing and shaving in saltwater, but it's all you get. The food is poor but don't think that I will starve.

Not much to write about, the censor will cut anything interesting out.

Love,
Dwight

*V-Mail transmission from Dwight to his parents from sea...
somewhere in the Pacific.*

20 May 1945

Dear Folks:

Finally got unloaded off of the boat and got on land again, certainly seems good to walk around and pick up a little dust.

[...]

almost as good as you get in the states. Have cots to sleep on and live in tents with [...]

Envelope:

T/3 Dwight E. Morgrove 17078445
939th Ord (HAM) Co.
A.P.O. 244 % Postmaster
San Francisco Calif.

U.S. ARMY
POSTAL SERVICE
1945 MAY 22
244

PASSED BY
U 49972 S
ARMY EXAMINER

Mrs Earl Morgrove
Gordon
Nebraska

May 20th 1945

T/3 Dwight E. Margrave
937 th Ord (HAM) Co.
Apo. 244 C/O Postmaster
San Francisco, Calif.

Marianas

Dear Folks:

Finally got unloaded off of the boat and got on land again. It certainly seems good to walk around and kick up a little dust.

I am in the Marianas and it isn't such a bad place. I have only been here two nights but it seems to be cool at night but pretty hot in the daytime. So far the food has been good. Almost as good as you get in the states. We have cots to sleep on and live in tents with wooden floors. We have shower baths, but the water is pretty scarce so we can't use too much.

We have several bunches of bananas hanging up in our tent that we picked and are waiting for them to ripen. They grow most everywhere around here.

We can watch the big B-29's leave here with loads of bombs to dump on Tokyo and we see them come back. It takes quite a while to make a round trip. Some of them seem to leave most every day. I haven't been to the airport yet, but will try to get up there some of these days.

There are a few Japs left in the hills here but they stay in caves and are almost impossible to get out. They don't bother anything, only they try to sneak down and steal food at night. But usually some guard kills them. They are dangerous if you would get up near their caves, but that is restricted, and no one is allowed to get near that area. I guess they have men trying to hunt them out all the time, but it is almost impossible. About the only danger is the dud shells and mines that have been left from the invasion. There are lots of ammo and Jap bones left laying around.

I will write again soon. I am OK and don't think I will mind it much here.

As Ever,
Dwight

> *"We can watch the **big B-29's** leave here with loads of bombs to dump on Tokyo."*

AS EVER, *Dwight*

MARIANA ISLANDS

B-29 Superfortress 'Enola Gay' landing after the atomic bombing mission on Hiroshima, Japan. Tinian, Marianas Islands. August 6, 1945.

SAIPAN

Circa May, 1945

Saipan is the largest island of the Northern Mariana Islands, a commonwealth of the United States located in the western Pacific Ocean.

The battle of Saipan was a battle of the Pacific campaign of WWII fought on the island of Saipan from the 15th of June to July 9th 1944. The US 2nd Marine Division, 4th Marine Division and the Army's 27th Infantry Division defeated the 43rd Infantry Division of the Imperial Japanese Army.

The loss of Saipan, with the deaths of at least 29,000 troops and heavy civilian casualties left the Japanese archipelago within the range of the United States Army Air Force B-29 bombers.

Dear Folks-

I am glad you got to meet my wife and think she is O.K. I do to-

Things are not so bad out here, not much to write about, the food has been good and have good living quarters, [obscured by envelope]
room [obscured]
is quite [obscured]
not th[obscured]
malar[obscured]

In [obscured]
I have [obscured]
my get [obscured]
ready [obscured]
just [obscured]
it wou[obscured]
bread fruit and papayas
that are supposed to be good

Envelope:
T/3 W.E. Morgrove 17028445
37 Ord (HAM) Co.
APO 244 % P.M.
S.F. Calif.

U.S. ARMY
244
MAY 29
1945
POSTAL SERVICE

PASSED BY
U 49972 S
ARMY EXAMINER

Mrs Earl Morgr[ove]
Gordon
Nebraska

T/3 W.E. Morgrove 17028445
37 Ord (HAM) Co

May 28th 1945

T/3 Dwight E. Margrave
937th Ord (HAM) Co.
Apo. 244 C/O Postmaster
San Francisco, Calif.

Marianas

Dear Folks:

I am glad you got to meet my wife and think she is OK. I do to.

Things are not so bad out here. There is not much to write about. The food has been good and we have good living quarters. They are building a shower room in our area. There are quite a few mosquitoes, but not the kind that have malaria.

In our tent we have nine bunches of bananas hanging up getting ripe. They are almost ready to eat now, if we just had some thick cream it would be OK. There is also breadfruit and papayas that are supposed to be good but don't believe I want any.

We are a little ahead of you folks; we had corn on the cob for dinner a few days ago. I don't know where it came from.

Dad, I will tell you a story about one of these natives. They are prisoners and get to run loose in the day, and work here and there. One of the fellows walked up to this native and reached in his pocket and pulled out a sharp knife and handed it to this native and told him Hari Kari. The native said "me no soldier me farmer." I guess he didn't want to join his ancestors so bad.

That is about all tonight.

As Ever,
Dwight.

"I am glad you got to meet my wife and think she is OK. I do to."

Dear Sis:

I am getting along O.K. over here, don't work ha[rd?] [ ] hard and get good food. [ ] have tents to sleep in [ ]ing The climate isn't so bad although it rains ev[ery] but the sun will [ ] and dry [ ]

T/3 L.E. Morgrove 17073445
937 Ord H.A.M. Co
APO 244 % P.M.
S.F. Cal.

Mrs Glen Keyser
Gordon
Nebr.

PASSED BY
49972
U.S.
ARMY EXAMINER

[ ] that you [ ]
[ ] were about
to go back to Denver with [ ]

T/3 L.E. Morgrove 17073445
937 Ord (HAM) C[o]

May 30th 1945

T/3 Dwight E. Margrave
937th Ord (HAM) Co.
Apo. 244 C/O Postmaster
San Francisco, Calif.

Marianas

Dear Sis,

I am getting along OK over here. I don't work too hard and get good food and have tents to sleep in. The climate isn't so bad; although it rains every day but the sun will be out and dry everything off a few minutes later.

Sis, how is Carol Ann getting along? I bet she can walk by now. Does she still stay awake at night and sleep all day? Can she talk a few words yet?

Irean said she was over to Gordon, and saw you folks and that you and Marion were about to go back to Denver with her. It might be all right if you want to. I have been getting a little mail lately. I think I will start writing more and maybe I will get more letters. I really appreciate a letter over here.

I have been over most of the island. There are roads everywhere; but I have never been up to the B-29 base yet. I may go up there next Sunday, From the news we get they are sure making it hot for Tokyo.

Well this is about all for now, so guess I will crawl between the blankets.

As Ever,
Dwight

> "*I have been getting little mail lately. I think **I will start writing more** and maybe I will get more letters.*"

Saipan
June 12-44

Dear Folks:

At last we are allowed to give our location, which is Saipan, you can find it on most any map of ... If you folks ...

Envelope:
Pfc L.E. Morgrove 17078445
93rd Chm (HTM) Co
APO 244 % Postmaster
San Francisco, Cal.

U.S. ARMY POSTAL SERVICE 1945 JUN 14 244

PASSED BY U.S. 49972 ARMY EXAMINER

Mrs Earl Morgrove
Gordon
Nebr.

June 12th 1945

T/3 Dwight E. Margrave
937th Ord (HAM) Co.
Apo. 244 C/O Postmaster
San Francisco, Calif.

Saipan

Dear Folks,

At last we are allowed to give our location, which is Saipan. You can find it on most any map of the Pacific. If you folks know of any of the fellows that I know from home that have an APO 244 or in Saipan let me know and I will look them up some Sunday.

I don't mind it here at all only there isn't much of any thing to do except go swimming or ride around the island. There are roads most everywhere. We have a softball team that doesn't amount to much. Ben Durrer is catcher and I think about the best player.

I took a swimming test yesterday, everyone had to. I swam 100 yards with all your clothes, steel helmet and shoes, 100 yards with a life jacket and 100 yards free style. I made all of them but wouldn't want to go much further with all my clothes on because it gets to be a long drag. I don't think you could possibly get your second wind with a life preserver on.

I am working in a shop for another outfit, rebuilding axles, not a bad job but it would get tiresome if you had to do the same thing for the duration.

I hear from Irean most every day. That is, I may get four letters one day and then skip four or five days. I don't think she is too well satisfied with her job.

Time for me to go to bed.

As Ever,
Dwight

> "I hear from Irean most every day. That is, I may get four letters one day and then skip four or five days."

SAIPAN

Photo taken by Dwight, 103 Area Saipan 1945.

DWIGHT EARL MARGRAVE
A SOLDIER'S JOURNEY THROUGH WWII

1945

Photo taken by Dwight, "Fox Hole" 1945.

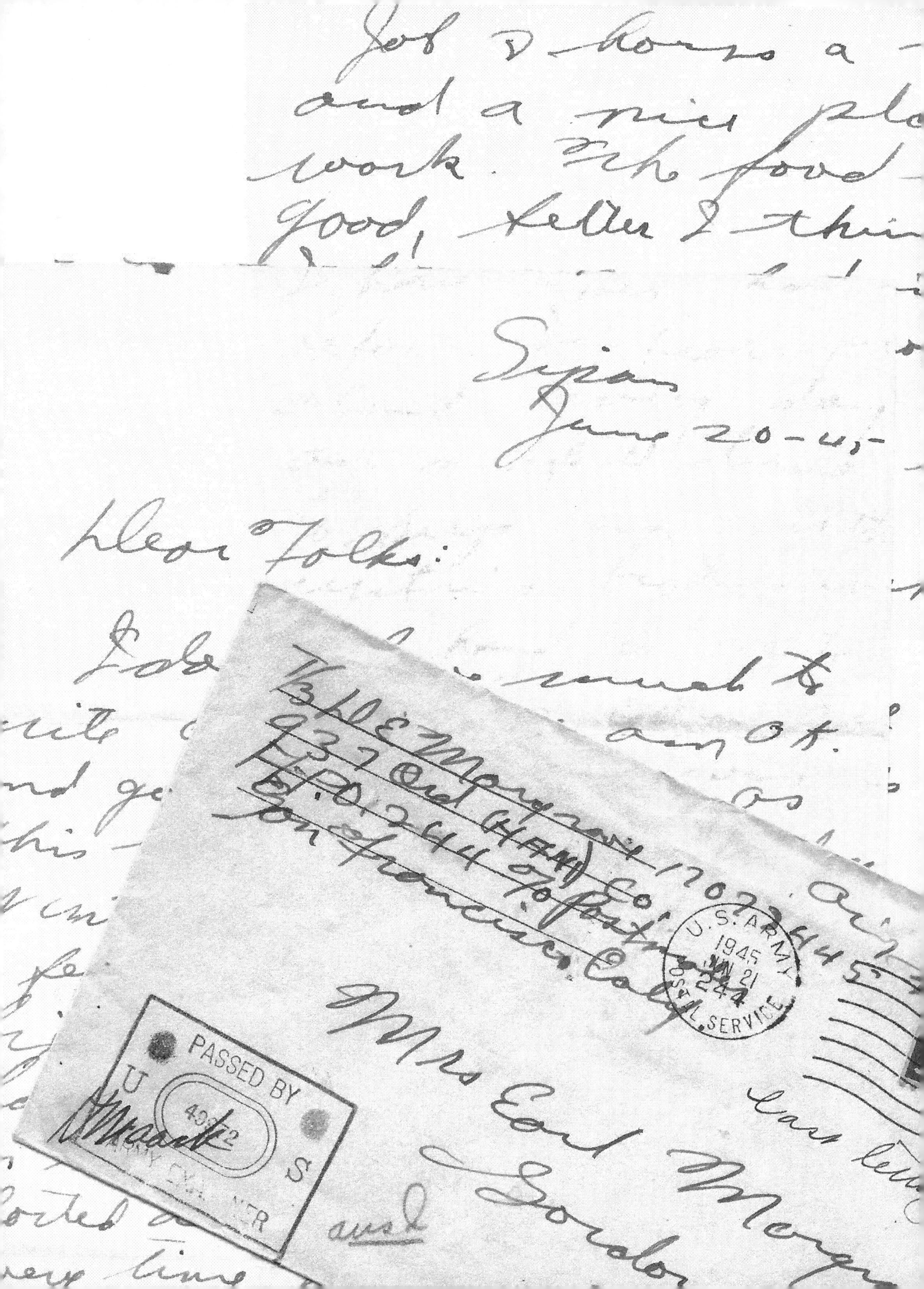

Job & hours a [...]
and a nice pl[...]
work. The food [...]
good, better I thin[...]

Sipan
June 20-45-

Dear Folks:

[envelope:]
Sgt P.E. Morgan 120[...]
937 Ord (HAM) Co. A[...]
APO 244 % postm[...]
San Francisco Calif.

Mrs Earl Morgan
[...] Gordon

PASSED BY
49 [...]
U.S. ARMY EXAMINER

U.S. ARMY
1945
JUN 21
POSTAL SERVICE

DWIGHT EARL MARGRAVE
A SOLDIER'S JOURNEY THROUGH WWII

#92

June 20th 1945

T/3 Dwight E. Margrave
937th Ord (HAM) Co.
Apo. 244 C/O Postmaster
San Francisco, Calif.

Saipan

Dear Folks:

I don't have much to write about but I am OK and getting along fine, as this isn't such a bad place.

I went to the dentist a few days ago. I had a tooth filled. That dentist sure had me bouncing around in the chair. The drill was shorted and it would shock me every time he would get it in my mouth. After we discovered what it was and fixed the short it wasn't so bad then.

I have been working in a shop for another company. Not a bad job, ten hours a day, and a nice place to work. The food is still good, better I think than I have ever had in the army before.

I hear from Irean about every day. I have an awful time trying to keep up with this letter writing, as I never was much of a hand to write.

I hope you are all O.K. and this war is over soon.

As Ever,
Dwight

"That dentist *sure had me* bouncing around *in the chair.*"

Sipon
July 1 - 45 -

Dear Folks:

I was very disappointed with you when I heard that you had one of my letters published in the paper - Please don't ever do that again, because I am notin this d—— army for any publicity - and on top of that Chet will have me in the doghouse with my wife - Oh well I guess there is nothing to do but forgett it.

Don't have much to write about, as the censor is very strict. Has been pretty hot here but always cool at

July 1st 1945

T/3 Dwight E. Margrave
937th Ord (HAM) Co.
Apo 244 C/O Postmaster
San Francisco, Calif.

Saipan

Dear Folks:

I was very disappointed with you when I heard that you had one of my letters published in the paper.

Please don't ever do that again, because I am not in this damn army for any publicity—and on top of that you will have me in the doghouse with my wife.

Oh well, I guess there is nothing to do but forget it.

I don't have much to write about, as the censor is very strict. It has been pretty hot here, but always cool at night. The food is still good and I am not working too hard. So I guess that is all you can expect here.

Dad, how is the crop on the farm this summer? Has it rained yet? Do you and Charley and Pat still play cards and pool down in the Masonic Temple? The C.13s. have a lodge here on the island. Another fellow and I planned to go but didn't make it.

This is about all I have to write for now, so hope that you are all OK.

As Ever,
Dwight

> *"I was very disappointed with you when I heard that you had one of my letters published in the paper."*

JULY 16ᵀᴴ 1945

Alamogordo, New Mexico

*Photograph of the first atomic bomb taken
nine seconds after the initial Trinity detonation.*

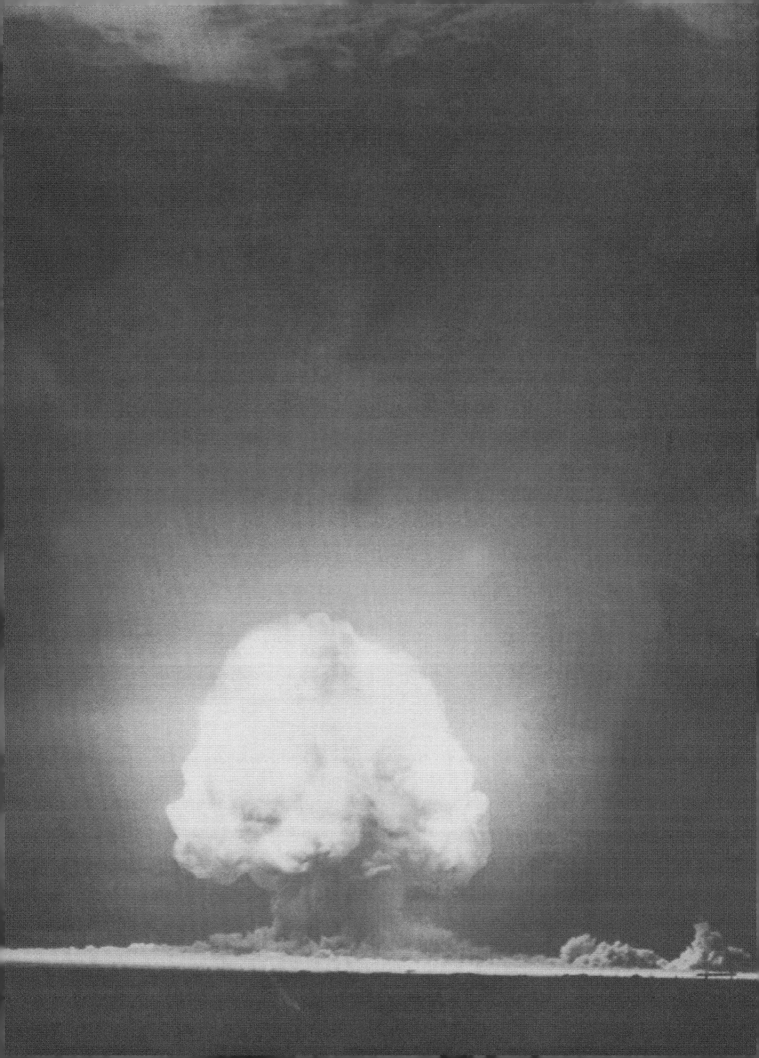

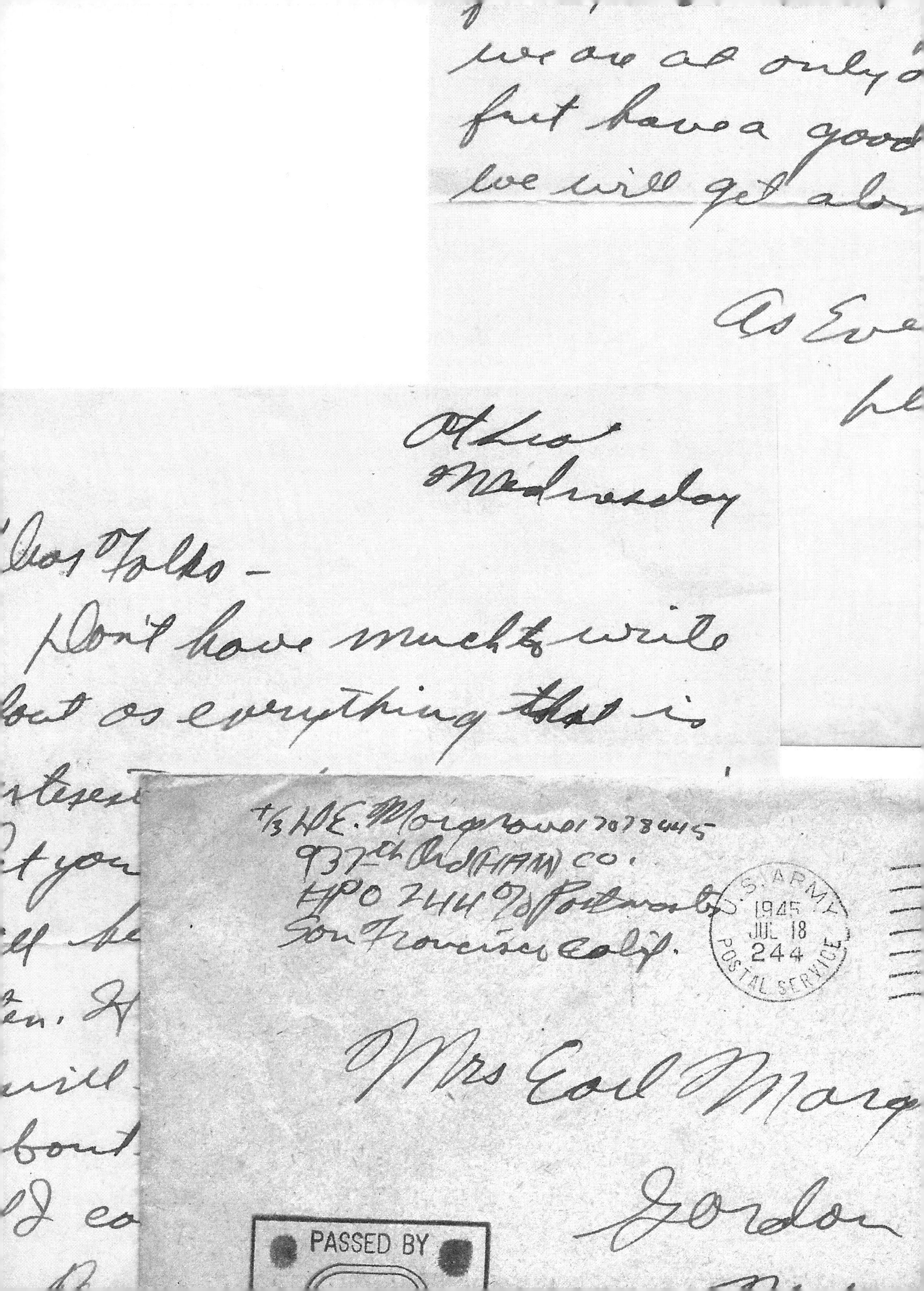

we are at only [?]
but have a good
we will get alo[ng]

As Eve[r]
L[ove]

Atu[?]
Wednesday

Dear Folks -

Don't have much to write
about as everything that is
interest[ing]
[...]

T/3 W. E. Morgrow 70784445
937th Ord (HAM) Co.
APO 244 % Postmaster
San Francisco Calif.

U.S. ARMY
1945
JUL 18
244
POSTAL SERVICE

Mrs Earl Marg[row]
Gordon

PASSED BY

DWIGHT EARL MARGRAVE
A SOLDIER'S JOURNEY THROUGH WWII

#94

July 18th 1945

T/3 Dwight E. Margrave
937th Ord (HAM) Co.
Apo 244 C/O Postmaster
San Francisco, Calif.

At Sea

Dear Folks,

Don't have much to write about as everything that is interesting the censors won't let you write. So these letters will be short and not very often.

If we land somewhere I will let you know all about the trip and our destination if I can.

I received mail yesterday. I got a letter from Mom and Marjorie. I was glad to hear from you. I hope sis likes it up at Rushville.

Don't worry about me, as I am OK and getting along fine. I can't tell you where we are at, only at sea. We have a good ship and we will get along OK.

As Ever,
Dwight

> *"If we land somewhere I will let you know all about the trip and our destination if I can."*

RYUKYU ISLANDS

Circa 1945

The Ryukyu Islands, also know as the Nansei Islands, are a chain of Japanese Islands that stretch southwest from Kyushu to Taiwan. They form the boundary between the East China Sea and the Philippine Sea.

The islands include the Osumi, Tokaka, Amami, Okinawa and Sakishaama Islands. The largest islands are mostly high islands and the smaller islands mostly coral.

The battleship USS Idaho shelling Okinawa on April 1st, 1945. Courtesy National Photo Archives.

AS EVER, *Dwight*

AUG 6TH 1945

Hiroshima

August 6th, 1945, an American B-29 bomber dubbed Enola Gay dropped an atomic bomb (Little Boy) on the Japanese city of Hiroshima. It was the first time a nuclear weapon had been deployed in warfare and the bomb immediately killed 80,000 people. Tens of thousands more would later die of radiation exposure.

...l trip on the...
...what ever. Weather...
...all the time...
...is any location as...
...I am at only north...
...quator and west of...
...national date line...
...isos are pretty rough...
...a given date

...ly ports a...
...area of p...
...nnel on b...
...taking s...
...ath compe...
...shower...
...next lo...

J.E. Morrow 17078445
...Cn (H)(T)(N)CO
...901 ℅ Postmaster
...Francisco Calif

Mrs Earl Morrow
Gordon

Rec'd Aug 8 45

August 8th 1945

T/3 D.E. Margrave
937th Ord (HAM) Co.
APO 244 C/O Postmaster
San Francisco, Calif.

Unknown Location

Dear Folks,

We arrived here OK. I had a swell trip on the ship. No trouble what ever. The weather was good all the time.

I can't give any location as to where I am at, only north of the equator and west of the International Date Line. The censors are pretty rough at present; we can't even date our letters.

I haven't much of a let up here. We are setting up tents and fixing up the area at present. We have all canned and dehydrated food to eat.

I just finished taking a hot shower up at a bath company. All they do is set up showers and delousing. I wasn't lousing but sure pretty dirty.

I will write again soon. Probably before long I can let you know a little more about everything here.

I had mail waiting when we arrived.

As Ever
Dwight

> *"I can't give any location as to where I am at, only north of the equator and west of the International Date Line."*

AS EVER, *Dwight*

AUG 9TH 1945

Nagasaki

Three days later, August 9th, 1945, another atomic bomb (Fat Man) was dropped on the Japanese city Nagasaki, instantly killing a further 40,000 people. Again, over time the number of fatalities increased considerably as the devastating effects of a nuclear fallout were played out for the world to see.

AMERICAN RED CROSS

In the Ryukyus
August 12-45

Dear Folks -

Have just received news that the war is over officially. Do not know if that is right or not but do hope that it is. We heard over the radio over about two days ago and there was certainly a celebration over this Island. It was about 9 P.M. and ... news came over the radio ... like every gun

---

T/3 D. E. Margrave 17098445
937 Ord H M Co.
A.P.O. 901 % Postmaster
San Francisco Calif.

Mrs Earl Margrave

August 12th 1945

T/3 D.E. Margrave
937th Ord (HAM) Co.
A.P.O. 901 C/O Postmaster
San Francisco, Calif.

In the Ryukyu's

Dear Folks,

Have just received news that the war is over officially. I do not know if that is right or not but do hope that it is.

We heard the war was over about two days ago and there was certainly a celebration over this Island. It was about 9:00pm and the news came over the radio. It seemed like every gun and flare on the Island were in the air at the same time. All the searchlights on the aircraft guns were in operation. It beat any of the Fourth of July celebrations that you could see. Everything quieted down in about an hour and since then is just the same as always.

If I don't get stuck in the army of occupation I may have a chance of getting home by the end of the year. I have lots of hopes but they may not materialize. The last three years in the army has been an awful long time.

I haven't had much mail since we arrived here but I did get the pictures of Carol Ann. She is sure growing. I bet she is awful cute and probably talking a little.

I am sending a little money and a couple of Jap powder bags. We get payed in the military currency and the other is genuine Jap money. Ten Sen is a penny. One Yen is a dime. I can hardly count the stuff. There isn't any thing to buy but cigarettes and candy at the P.X.

I think that new bomb had a lot to do with the end of the war. I hope it is over for good.

As Ever,
Dwight

> *"I think that new bomb had a lot to do with the end of the war. I hope it is over for good."*

Japanese Soldier Powder Bags.

Japanese Money sent back to Dwight's parents.

The super battleship Yamato explodes after persistent attacks from US aircraft, April 7th 1945. (National Photo Archives)

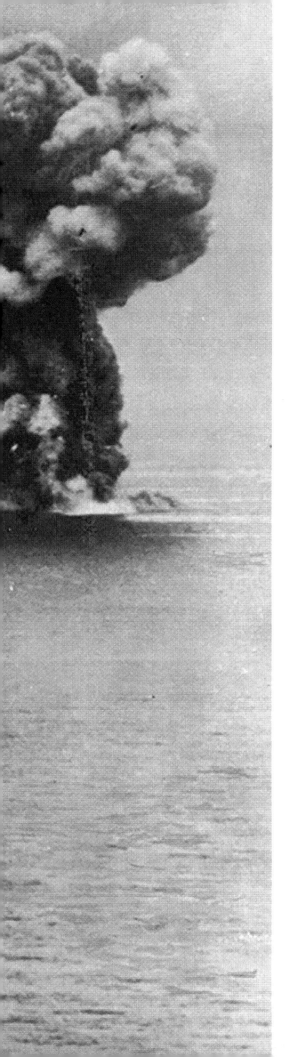

DWIGHT EARL MARGRAVE
A SOLDIER'S JOURNEY THROUGH WWII

OKINAWA JAPAN

Circa 1945

The initial invasion of Okinawa on April 1st, 1945 was the largest amphibious assault in the Pacific Theater of Word War II. The 82 day battle lasted from April 1st until June 22nd, 1945. Finally the US 10th Army overcame the last major pockets of the Japanese resistance on the Okinawa Island ending one of the bloodiest battles in WWII.

After a long campaign of island hopping, the Allies were planning to use Kadera Air Base on the large island of Okinawa as a base for Operation Downfall, the planned invasion of the Japanese home islands, 340 miles away.

On July 16th, 1945 the United States successfully tested an atomic bomb in the desert of New Mexico.

After dropping two of these devastating weapons on Hiroshima on August 6th, 1945 and on Nagasaki on August 9th, 1945, Japan surrendered.

AS EVER, *Dwight*

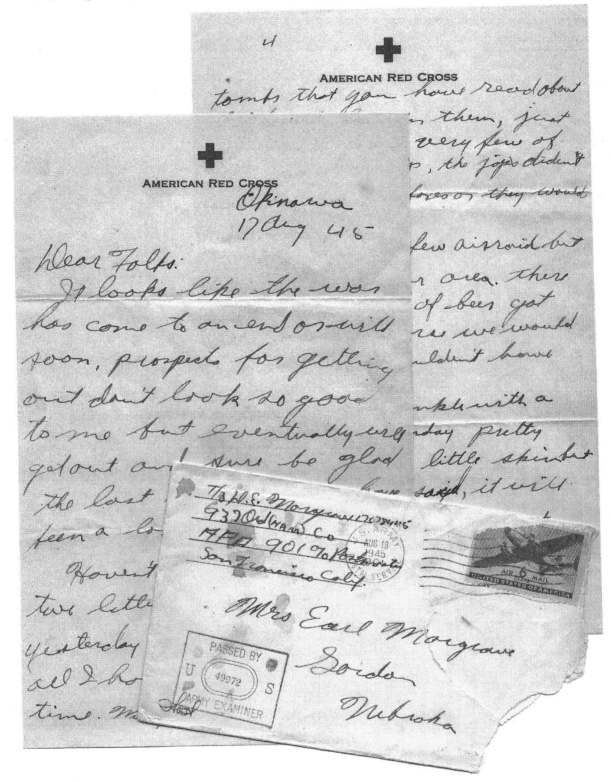

"*There was a ship load of beer that got hit, which of course we would like to have.*"

August 17th 1945

T/3 D.E. Margrave
937th Ord (HAM) Co.
APO 901 C/O Postmaster
San Francisco, Calif.

Dear Folks:

It looks like the war has come to an end or will soon. Prospects for getting out don't look so good to me but eventually I will get out and sure be glad. The last three years have been a long time.

I haven't had much mail: two letters from Irean yesterday, but that is all I have had for some time. I will probably hit a batch some of these days.

At last we can tell where we are at, Okinawa, and can't say that I like it. I haven't been all over the island, but what I have seen of it, it is all about the same. There was once a city of Noha, and now it is just nothing, There is not one building in one piece. There are shell holes and rubble everywhere. There just isn't anything that hasn't been torn upon.

There are a few Japs but not many I don't think.

The climate isn't so bad, but when it rains this clay gets slick and your feet get so much mud on them you can't hardly get around.

We have a bunch of "gooks," Jap women that work around the area. They carry lumber, break rock, cut grass and so forth. There were some hogs running loose around here, but they are all gone now. The "gooks" catch them and take them back to their camp. They ran one down and beat it to death with clubs and shovels yesterday. I bet it was sure good meat.

I have seen some of the tombs that you have read about, but haven't been in them, just full of old bones. Very few of them are torn up, the Japs didn't use them for pillboxes or they would have been.

We have had a few air raids, but none close to our area. There was a ship load of beer that got hit, which of course we would have liked to have: couldn't have hit something else.

I burned my ankle with a steam hose yesterday. It's pretty sore and I lost a little skin, but as Harry Hibbord said, "it will grow back." Otherwise I am OK and hope all of you folks are the same.

As Ever,
Dwight

AS EVER, *Dwight*

August 23rd 1945

T/3 D.E. Margrave
937th Ord (HAM) Co.
APO 901 C/O Postmaster
San Francisco, Calif.

#98

Okinawa

Dear Sis:

Was glad to get your letter, but sorry to hear about the flood at home. It seems like that there has been a lot of high water there in the last few years. It will sure make lots of work cleaning out the basement.

I have some pretty good news. Some of the men are to be transferred out of the company and think and hope that I will be one. This outfit isn't very good so it would be a pleasure to get to go. They will probably go into companies going to Japan or Korea. I can't see any hope of getting out of the army in the next six months and may be longer.

How is Carol Ann? I bet she is cute now and probably into everything.

I hear from Irean often and she is getting along OK.

This is about all for now. I sure am glad the war is over, and wish I was discharged.

Love,
Dwight

*"I sure am glad **the war is over**, and wish I was discharged."*

AMERICAN RED CROSS

Okinawa
Aug 23 - 45

Sis:

was glad to get your [letter]
but sorry to hear
[abou]t the flood at home,
[seems] like that there has
[been] a lot of high water
in the last few years.
[It w]ill sure make lots of
[wor]k cleaning out the
[base]ment.

[We h]ave some pretty good
[news], some of the men
[are] to be transferred out of
[the] company and I think
[& ho]pe that I will be
[one]. This outfit isn't

[...] would be a
[...]. Probably
[...] days going
[...]. Can't see
[...] of the
[...] months
[...] but
[...] and probably
[...] after
[...] O.K.
[...]
[...] discharged.

Love,
[R.]

AMERICAN RED CROSS Sept 3 - 45

Dear Folks -
 Hit the jackpot today
three letters, two from Jean
and one from dad, sure
glad to get some letters.
Don't get much news

T/3 H.R. Margrave 17078444 ?
937th Ord (HAM) Co
APO 180 % Postmaster
San Francisco Calif.

Mrs Earl Margrave
Gordon
Nebraska

PASSED BY
49972
U S
ARMY EXAMINER

or four days old. By the
— to carry the water

September 3rd 1945

T/3 D.E. Margrave
937th Ord (HAM) Co.
APO 901 C/O Postmaster
San Francisco, Calif.

Okinawa

Dear Folks,

Hit the jackpot today; three letters, two from Irean and one from Dad. I was sure glad to get some letters. We don't get much news here only a little on the radio that is the local station here and
the Stars and Stripes, a paper published for the armed forces. It is usually three or four days old by the time we get it.

This is certainly a disagreeable place. The war may be over but you can't tell it here. We are working hard and long hours and it is so muddy most of the tine. It is almost impossible to walk or do anything else.

We have to move from where we are to a new area about a half mile away. Just because some officer had a brainstorm. We were just getting this area fixed up a little. We have floors in our tents, ditches to carry the water away and some sand hauled in to cover the mud.

I am thoroughly disgusted with this army and can't get out too soon to suite me, but it doesn't look like I have a chance for some time.

Irean is getting along fine and I hope that Marion is also.

I will have 47 points the 13th of September but that isn't nearly enough. I think it will be lowered again in the next three or four months.

I hope it is. Well, time for bed.

As Ever,
Dwight

> "The war may be over but you can't tell it here."

AMERICAN RED CROSS

Okinawa
Sept 9 – 45

Dear Folks –

No more censoring of mail now so we can write anything we please. Lots of things I —

T/3 W. E. Margrave 17078445
937 Ord (HAM) Co.
A.P.O. 180 % Postmaster
San Francisco Calif.

Longest letter ever received from Dwight — no censor on it.

Mrs Earl Margrave
Gordon
Nebraska

about two — from shore and wrote Dwight

September 9th 1945

T/3 D.E. Margrave
937th Ord (HAM) Co.
A.P.O. 180 C/O Postmaster
San Francisco, Calif.

Okinawa

Dear Folks,

No more censoring of mail now so we can write anything we please. Lots of things I have been wanting to tell you about but couldn't.

We left Saipan and were on the ship about three weeks coming on over here; but for two weeks we just sat in the harbor about two miles from shore and waited for a convoy to be made up. There were about seventy-five ships and several destroyers for escorts. It looked like enough ships steering through the waters to make an invasion.

Our ship was an "L.S.T." Landing Ship Tank. It is one of those that has the big door in front and runs up to the beach and drops the door down and then you drive your truck off. It was a good trip, no trouble at all.

This area we have moved in was sure muddy and dirty, dead Japs laying most everywhere and they sure did stench. In fact this end of the island is all that way. We threw gasoline on all of the bodies around here and burned them. Some of them had hand grenades in their pockets and sure made some of the fellows take off when they blew up.

We are about three miles from Noha, which was a city of about 100,000. Now there isn't one building standing. It was a bad smelling place, but now it has been pretty well leveled off with bulldozers. The hills around here are nothing but shell holes. I don't think that there is over a 100 foot square that hasn't been hit by a big shell or bomb.

Don't know when we or rather I will get to come home, but think it will be sometime. I have only 48 points and there isn't any transportations back to the states. Sometimes I think that the big shots don't want to send us back as soon as possible. There are probably 1,500 ships in the harbor around the island, but they say they are loaded and were waiting to invade Japan. Now that is not necessary. They still have the cargo and no place to go with it. It will eventually get straightened out.

We have been working hard getting vehicles ready to go to Japan. They have to be painted and fully equipped. They are moving in here fully equipped and will put on some pretty fancy

Landing craft to supply U.S. forces on Okinawa, 13 days after the initial invasion. Beyond are U.S. battlewagons, cruisers and destroyers. April 13, 1945.

parades and show off. The Japs will see more tanks and equipment than they ever saw before and will realize that they never had a chance.

The first men to go in were from here and all of them had new uniforms. They were all shinned up and had to be 6' foot tall or over. The end came so quick that we were not fully prepared for victory.

One division was brought up here by air from the Philippines. Some of the planes were flying around waiting to land when the Japs made their last air raid here. They never bombed very close to us. They were always after the ships and airfield, although we saw them a few nights.

I wanted Bill Williams address. I thought that he might be here and I might be able to get to see him if he is on this island. We can get all over it, but the roads are not too good. It would be good to see someone from home and then we could both talk about how we would like to be back.

I hear from Irean about every day. Wish I was back to enjoy married life.

As Ever,
Dwight

P.S. This is a pretty long letter for me to write. Don't think I am sick because I am not.

AMERICAN RED CROSS

Okin[awa]
Sept 2

Dear Folks:

Received some mail
last few days the first
some time, mail got m[ixed]
up don't know just wh[at]
happen - typhoon blew th[at]
office —

[address portion:]
[illegible] 12078445
Co.
[Post]master
[San Francis]co Calif.

Mrs Earl Morgan

September 25th 1945

T/3 D.E. Margrave
937th Ord (HAM) Co.
A.P.O. 180 C/O Postmaster
San Francisco, Calif.

Okinawa

Dear Folks,

Received some mail the last few days. The first for some time, the mail got mixed up. I don't know just what did happen. The typhoon blew the post office down. Things were all mixed up for the last two weeks. We had a bad storm. It blew tents down and ships clear up on dry land. It just raised cain in general, lots of rain with the wind.

Work has been slowing down in the shop the last two weeks. I hope it continues and the faster they get this equipment, tanks, trucks and guns dumped in the ocean the sooner we will be home. The war is over. I am getting more anxious to get back to the states than ever. They have started dumping a few junk tanks in now, some that are shot up or worn out.

We are sure getting poor food, hash and stew at least twice a day. No fresh food. It is all canned or dehydrated. The cooks are poor also. We get out and steal bacon and once in a while a few eggs or potatoes and fry up a meal in the evenings. Ben Durrer and I are the head cooks in our tent.

We have a bunch of Jap prisoners working around here now and we make them work too. They stay outside and pound rock while the guards stay inside and look out. Some of them don't have hardly any clothes, some bare footed. I saw one with only one shoe. They aren't in too good of shape. They are not very strong and some pretty badly scared up from bullets. All their wounds aren't healed yet but they work just the same. They are treated better than our prisoners were, but still not very good.

Irean said that she had a good time at home and took in the county fair. I wish I could have been there also.

I have been operating a bulldozer for about a week. I haven't been in the shop.

Dad, that little tractor must be all right. I will overhaul it for you next spring.
I hope I can be home by then.

As Ever,
Dwight

Okinawa
Oct. 2-45

Dear Folks:-

Will drop you a few lines today and let you know that I am o.k. but still want to get out of the army, don't think I'll ever be a professional

[envelope:]
T/3 R.E. Morgan 17078445
937 Ord (HAM) Co.
A.P.O. 180 % Postmaster
San Francisco Calif.

Mrs Earl Morgan
Gordon
Nebr.

with our money now,

all well –
As Ever,
Alvright

October 2nd 1945

T/3 D.E. Margrave
937th Ord (HAM) Co.
A.P.O. 180 C/O Postmaster
San Francisco, Calif.

Okinawa

Dear Folks,

Will drop you a few lines today and let you know that I am OK but still want to get out of the army. I don't think I could ever be a professional soldier. It is "No" career for me.

So the baby got in the eggs and started scrambling them? Well if she starts scrambling eggs at that age, I don't know, but she will probably be a good cook.

We are sure mixed up with our money now. We use that stuff like I sent you and get our pay in it. We can't spend American money. Then we had to turn it all back in and about two days later we got the same stuff back only half again as much more.

Dad, I guess that is inflation. We have more money now but it takes more to buy a pack of cigarettes.

We had ice tea for dinner today, the first cold drink of anything since we left Saipan. It sure tasted good.

I have been operating a bulldozer. I sure got stuck this morning. I fell off of a bank about 5 feet high and the tractor lit right on the blade that is in front of it. It didn't hurt anything but nearly threw me, bad as Ben Robert's horse.

Soldiers clearing Okinawa with Thompson submachine guns after heavy shelling by the U.S. Navy. (National Archives Photo)

Have you read about the tombs that the natives have here? I went into some of them the other day. They are all made out of concrete and have a hole about two feet square. You go in the hole and there isn't much room, not enough to stand up and there are big vases full of bones.

The natives take their dead in there and leave them until most of the meat rots off of the bones and then they go in and scrape them of the remainder off and use it for fertilizer, and put the bones in the vase with the scull.

Each one has Jap writing on it but I don't know what it says, probably their name. Some pretty vases but the army won't let the fellows take them. They are the only things that were left on this island that were not blown or torn up. The Japs didn't destroy them or use them for pill boxes. I don't know why. Some of them smell pretty bad.

My ankle has one little scab left to peal off and then it will be OK. It takes even a little scratch a long time to heal here, but doesn't seem to be much infection. Thatis why they have to evacuate the wounded out of here. Lots of skin diseases, pimples, rash, ringworm and such. I haven't had any, so I will knock on wood.

Bed time for now. I hope you are all well.

As Ever,
Dwight

Okinawa
Oct 14 - 45

Dear Folks:-

Suppose by now you have heard all about the typhoon that we had here. Don't know what the papers said but truly it was really a bad storm.

I survived in good shape, only was wet for awhile and had wet blankets to sleep in. Our tent was one out of nine that didn't go down but it blew the rain through the canvas just like it was cheese cloth. The only reason our tent didn't go down is ___ over and broken in two.

The navy suffered a big loss.

As Ever
Dwight

October 14th 1945

T/3 D.E. Margrave
937th Ord (HAM) Co.
A.P.O. 180 C/O Postmaster
San Francisco, Calif.

Okinawa

Dear Folks:

Suppose by now you have heard all about the typhoon that we had here. I don't know what the papers said, but it was really a bad storm.

I survived in good shape. I was only wet for a while and had wet blankets to sleep in. Our tent was one out of nine that didn't go down, but it blew the rain through the canvas just like it was cheesecloth. The only reason our tent didn't go down is that we have a wooden door and three-foot sides made out of 2x12's and lots of 16" penny nails.

The storm began about noon and continued all night. The wind was up to 132 miles per hour and then the capes broke, but we are inland about two miles from the coast so didn't get quite as much wind. It blew down all of our shops. Some of them were made out of railroad rails and 4" inch pipe for studding and rafters with wooden roofs; but it tore them up just the same. It damaged lots of trucks that we had in the shop being repaired.

The rain with the wind was just like a high-pressure hose. It would just sting like hail when you were in it. Most of the fellows here slept in trucks and tanks that night, all different places. They went to the caves in the hill and in the tombs to sleep.

There must be nearly a hundred ships setting high and dry on the beach and rocks. All sizes, some turned over and broken in two.

The navy suffered a big loss in men and ships. I don't know how they will ever get a ship that weighs 20,000 tons off of solid rock and back in the water. I don't think that they can.

Personnel surveying the debris and the severely damaged USS Ocelot (IX-110) and USS Nestor (ARB-6) caused by Typhoon Louise at Buckner Bay, Okinawa, in October 1945.
(US Navy photo)

Nearly all of the tents on the island were destroyed, hospitals and all. Lots of planes were torn up or damaged. Some of the ships that were sunk had food and winter clothes, so we mostly run short of food. There is supposed to be only a weeks rations left on the island. They are flying it in B-29s now.

I haven't had any mail for about two weeks. I don't know what has happened. It looks like a letter would come through soon. Our post office blew away and mail bags also. So I don't suppose we will get all of our mail or that our letters will get home.

There is some talk of evacuating this island. I certainly hope so as it isn't a very good place. It rains so much; 120"-140" inches a year. We can see now why the Japs had so many caves: to get out of storms. What few houses are left we have often wondered why they are built the way they are 4x4 studding and the roof has a layer of bamboo poles about two inches of clay and tile roofing on top. But I guess that was so it wouldn't blow away.

One place on the beach there is a large oil tanker with two smaller ships on top of it. I don't want any more storms like that for a while. If we get another I think I will go to the caves even if I have to chase the Japs out first.

As Ever,
Dwight

> *"Our post office blew away and mail bags also. So I don't suppose we will get all of our mail or that our letters will get home."*

Okinawa
Nov-2-45.

Dear Folks:-

Just a few lines to let
[yo]u know that I am getting a-
long fine, that is as good
[as] possible here. Haven't
[ha]d any more typhoons lately
[an]d don't want any more.
[Ha]ve had lots of wet weather
[se]ems like it rains almost
[e]very day don't think the
[m]ud ever dries up, haven't
[se]en it dry as yet.
Chances for coming home

November 2nd 1945

T/3 D.E. Margrave
937th Ord (HAM) Co.
A.P.O. 180 C/O Postmaster
San Francisco, Calif.

Okinawa

Dear Folks,

Just a few lines to let you know that I am getting along fine. That is as good as possible here. We haven't had any More typhoons lately and we don't want any more. We have had lots of wet weather. It seems like it rains almost every day. I don't think the mud ever dries up. I haven't seen it dry as yet.

Chances for coming home don't look so good for a while, but I still have hopes. We are getting lots of replacements here: fellows with six months to one year in the army, but the men are not going home very fast.

The army is too slow with everything that they do, and things are so mixed up. There is so much red tape: it is a wonder that we ever won this war. It was certainly due to large numbers of men and equipment, not management.

It's probably getting pretty cold in Nebraska by now. I don't think it ever freezes here but it does get chilly at night. Our shower water seems like ice. We are building a heater to put in the tank.

We have a lot of new equipment in our mess hall; stolen, borrowed, and begged, most of it came from the navy. We have an ice cream machine just like Jim Sault's in Gordon. We have two large refrigerators, one electric and one has a jeep engine, a diesel burning stove, and an electric mixer, and a lot of other odds and ends.

We have the best equipped mess hall on the Island. The food has been much better, but we don't get too much fresh food as yet.

Mom, did you pay Dad what I owe him? If I have a $150 left send it to Irean. I have to buy a Christmas present so I will get her a diamond ring. All for now. Lights out.

As Ever,
Dwight

Sunday
Nov 11- 45

Dear Folks -
Received a couple of letters
and haven't answered them
but haven't had much to
write about, will have to tell
you about the weather, we had
one whole week with out any
rain, can't hardly believe it's
... yet but it did -

T/3 L.E. Margrave 120724445
937 Ord. HAM Co
APO 180 % Postmaster
San Francisco Calif

Mrs Earl Margrave
Gordon
Nebraska

Rec'd. Nov. 21
1945 Before
the day before
Thanksgiving

November 11th 1945

T/3 D.E. Margrave
937th Ord (HAM) Co.
A.P.O. 180 C/O Postmaster
San Francisco, Calif.

Okinawa

Dear Folks,

Received a couple of letters and I haven't answered them. I just haven't had much to write about only will have to tell you about the weather. We had one whole week without any rain. I can't hardly believe it really happened yet, but it did.

We listened to the football game today. Navy sure walked on Notre Dame. It comes in here on Sunday, as we are about a day ahead of you folks.

I received a Christmas package from Irean today, some canned food and olives; and you know how I like stuffed olives.

I built me a bed today. I made a frame out of two by four and stretched strips of old truck tubes across for springs. It works swell, if I can get a hold of a mattress now I will have something.

We are getting pretty well set here now. We have a good mess hall and the food is pretty good. We have hot water showers and a ball field but no time to play ball. We have been getting coral and sand over the area to get out of the mud. I couldn't get it for a long time; it all went on the roads and airfields.

They are sure trying hard to get men to reenlist in the army. They have talked lots of them here to sign up for one more year, but here is one that won't.

I am sending a few pictures taken on the island. I wish I knew as much about pictures as Marion, but I never did take much interest in them. Irean was going to send some film, but it hasn't come yet. It takes about two months to get a package unless it comes air mail.

It is about time for lights out, so I must try out my new bed. I just heard on the radio that it is ten below in North Dakota. You had better put more coal in the stoker box. It doesn't get down to freezing here.

As Ever,
Dwight

"They are sure trying hard to get men to reenlist in the army."

suppose you have heard about
in points, 56 points 21 years
years old or 3 kids — dam it!

T/3 HQ Marqeau 17098446
939 Ord H.A.M. Co
APO 13070 Postmaster
San Francisco Calif.

U.S. ARMY
NOV 20
1945
POSTAL SERVICE

Marjorie Keyser
Gordon
Nebr —

it is also getting
at nite, sometimes you
it would almost frost
the last time I saw her —
Will close for now

November 18th 1945

T/3 D.E. Margrave
937th Ord (HAM) Co.
A.P.O. 180 C/O Postmaster
San Francisco, Calif.

Okinawa

Dear Sis;

Suppose you have heard about the cut in points: 56 points and 4 years service, or 35 years old or 3 kids- dam it! I am just under the line; 47 points and 3 years 4 months of service, but I have hopes of making it out or at least being eligible by January 1st.

Everything is about the same here, only it hasn't been raining so much, the rainy season must be over. It is also getting chilly at night; sometimes you think it would almost frost.

So Carol Ann is getting some teeth; I bet she don't cry anymore about getting them than some of us do about having one pulled.

It is probably getting pretty cold by now isn't it? So you and Hank got some pheasants; I would sure like to set down to one all cooked and some good hot biscuits.

Sis, I hope Irean can cook as good as you. I get a letter from her about every day but don't write hardly that often. I never was much to write letters.

Sis, what will I do when I get out of the army? Do you have any suggestions? Well I won't worry much now. Do know that I won't sign up again.

Ben Denver got hit in the eye with a baseball and broke something. The pupil in one eye is about three times as large as the other and he can't see to well with it. Ben don't get a bit excited about it and was playing baseball again as soon as he got out of the hospital. The doctor said it would get all right.

I bet Carol Ann is about to run around and into everything by now. She was sure a cute little diver the last time I saw her.

I will close for now.

Love,
Brother

> "Sis, what will I do when I get out of the army?"

made out of st— of tin
tubes x.

Nov. 27- 45

Dear Folks -
Just a few lines to let you know that am getting along fine and still waiting on points or order to be

---

T/3 W.E. Margrave 17078445
937 QM H.F.M. Co /
APO 1809 Postmaster
San Francisco Calif.

U.S. ARMY POSTAL SERVICE NOV 28 1945

6¢ U.S. POSTAGE VIA AIR MAIL

Mrs Earl Margrave
Gordon
Nebr.

November 27th 1945

T/3 D.E. Margrave
937th Ord (HAM) Co.
A.P.O. 180 C/O Postmaster
San Francisco, Calif.

Okinawa

Dear Folks,

Just a few lines to let you know that I am getting along fine and still waiting for the points or age to be dropped low enough so that it will catch me. I will probably be eligible to leave the first of January, but then it will take about two months.

Another fellow and I were drafted into a pretty mean job. Some of the fellows around here had a still out in the hills. So the battalion commander picked this fellow and myself to go out in the hills and just wait until we found someone at the still and bring them in. We stayed out all night and the next morning saw two fellows. They broke and ran and got away. We fired a few shots but not at them. We didn't want to kill anyone.

It sure was a spooky place to stay at night. It was in an old Jap village full of caves, brush, stone walls and a few native huts. There has been Japs around there also. I don't know which I was the most scared of; the Japs or the moon shiners. They destroyed the still today so I don't think there will be any more of this watching; not if I can get out of it for sure.

I haven't been working very hard lately. We are getting more time off to play ball. Saturday afternoons and Sundays of course there isn't much to do in your time off only sleep. I have a good bed made out of strips of truck tubes woven like a mat and stretched, also a mattress, so I spend most of my spare time there, reading and sleeping.

It is bed time now.

Hope you are all OK.

As Ever,
Dwight

> "They broke and ran and got away. We fired a few shots but not at them. **We didn't want to kill anyone.**"

Okinawa
Dec 2 —

Dear Dad:

Just a few lines to let you know that I am getting along O.K. and still have [hopes]

of getting back to the States eventually, should be ela[ted?]

by the ti[me]

Mr Earl M[usgrove?]

December 2nd 1945

T/3 D.E. Margrave
937th Ord (HAM) Co.
A.P.O. 180 C/O Postmaster
San Francisco, Calif.

Okinawa

Dear Dad,

Just a few lines to let you know that I am getting along OK and still have hopes of getting back to the states eventually. I should be eligible by the first of the year. The transportations in awful slow here, in fact there are 18,000 on this island eligible waiting for ships.

Navy sure got beat by Army. I heard the broadcast at 3:00am this morning. I was on charge of quarters and had to be up all night. I had a ticket on a $2 pool on the total score but didn't win 80¢ pool.

There is an Okinawa Masonic club here on the island run by the navy and I am invited to attend. I will go up next Thursday night. It is just a get together and ice cream and donuts; it isn't really a lodge.

I will have to get to bed before the lights go out.

As Ever your son,
Dwight

> "There is an *Okinawa Masonic club* here on the island run by the navy and I am invited to attend."

Oct. 16- 45

Dear folks-

Only 9 more days until Christmas, time has been going pretty fast. Our radio announces here always says — more shipping days until Christmas as that is the big thing here is points and when we will get to — Only have to

December 16th 1945

T/3 D.E. Margrave
937th Ord (HAM) Co.
A.P.O. 180 C/O Postmaster
San Francisco, Calif.

Okinawa

Dear Folks,

Only nine more days until Christmas, time has been going pretty fast. Our radio announcer here always says nine more shipping days until Christmas as that is the big thing here, points and when we will get to go home.

We only have to work about six hours a day now and spend the rest of our time sleeping or just killing time.

I went crabbing today and got two big fellows six inches across the body and legs a foot long. We boiled them and had crab meat. It is good eating if you like sea food. It would sure been good in a salad with lettuce and mayonnaise. Our food here has been good and plenty of it, but I sure would like to get to eat some of Marion's hot biscuits.

The Army is awful slow getting men back. We still have 70 point men here, but believe that I will be back in February.

I won't send a request for a package as it takes two months for them to get here and I will be back by then if I am not mistaken. Thanks anyhow.

Time to go to bed.

Love,
Dwight

I am sending a few snaps-

Okinawa
Dec 19- 45

Dear Wad-
Received your letter today,
[...] the [...] pretty good
for a letter to go [...]

T/3 W.E. Musgrave 17078445
931 Ord H.A.M. Co
APO 18 0% Postmaster
San Francisco Calif.

DEC 21 1945

Mr. Earl Musgr[ave]
Gordon
Nebraska

December 19th 1945

T/3 D.E. Margrave
937th Ord (HAM) Co.
A.P.O. 180 % Postmaster
San Francisco, Calif.

Okinawa

Dear Dad,

Received your letter today mailed on the tenth. That's pretty good time for a letter to go nine thousand miles. I wish that I could get back as fast as a letter when I leave here. It takes from twenty to thirty days on a ship to make it. I think that I will get to leave sometime next month.

Am sure getting anxious to leave. This is sure a disagreeable place, and also I am pretty anxious to be with the wife. This being married and so damn far away isn't any good.

I don't know just what to do when I get out. It is hard to plan on anything when you don't just know what things are like; that is conditions there.

I don't see any reason to get excited as I am sure that there will be opportunities if one just looks for them and can see them.

Well Dad, it won't be too long until we can eat some of Mom's good cooking together again.

As Ever your son,
Dwight

> *"Well Dad, it won't be too long until we can eat some of Mom's good cooking together again."*

Dear Sis,

Received one package that [you] sent, the fruit cake, and it was [received]. Will [be]

...

T/3 W.E. Marquart 12078415
932 Ord H.M. Co,
A.P.O. 180 % Postmaster
San Francisco Calif.

Mrs Glen Key[s]
Gordon
Neb[r]

DEC 1945

December 22nd 1945

T/3 D.E. Margrave
937th Ord (HAM) Co.
A.P.O. 180 C/O Postmaster
San Francisco, Calif.

Okinawa

SEASONS GREETINGS
A WORLD APART UNITED IN HEART
MERRY CHRISTMAS AND HAPPY NEW YEAR CARD

Dear Sis:

Received one package that you sent, the fruit cake, and it was sure good. I will let you know if the others get here OK.

Carol sure must be getting to be a big girl, climbing on chairs and running around. I would like to see her. She sure has grown; that is, by looking at the picture you sent.

I still don't have enough points but may get out on length of service by February 1st that is eligible. I sure am tired of this rock.

Irean sent me two packages, and also has one on the way that had a bottle in it. I don't know if it will get here or not. Very little does.

Sis, I will be back by spring I hope.

As Ever,
Dwight

P.S. I took some pictures and will send them when they are

"I'm sure tired of this rock."

Christmas.

Dear Folks -

Have been wishing all day that Jean and I could have of been home for Christmas

[address block:]
D.E. Margrave 17078445
37 Ord. H.A.M. Co
A.P.O. 180 % Postmaster
San Francisco Calif.

U.S. ARMY
DEC 27
POSTAL SERVICE
1945

Mrs Earl Margrave
Gordon
Nebr.

December 27th 1945

T/3 D.E. Margrave
937th Ord (HAM) Co.
A.P.O. 180 C/O Postmaster
San Francisco, Calif.

Okinawa

Dear Folks,

Have been wishing all day that Irean and I could have been home for Christmas day and dinner. It has been a long time since I have been home. This is my 4th Christmas in the Army. Well next year I hope.

I had a good dinner today: turkey, potatoes & gravy, peas, corn, dressing, ice cream and minced pie, coffee and a bottle of beer, but it wasn't anything like mother's dinner. The turkey was cold and just the surroundings make a big difference, and then all of the food piled up in an old mess kit. There just isn't anyone that can cook like mom anyhow.

We just had a big argument about vacuums: whether there is such a thing or isn't. We get to arguing about some of the darnedest things around here. It passes time anyhow.

The troop movement is sure slow. They are not trying to get the soldiers home. The higher ups will loose their jobs if they do. I believe that is the big reason. I will send you a letter that has been passed around and let you folks see how they are doing. It gets me all riled up. There isn't anything to do but sweat it out.

All for now.

Love,
Dwight

> *"I have been wishing all day that Irean and I could have been home for Christmas day and dinner."*

Dwight returns home to Gordon, Nebraska, 1946.

1946
HEAD HOME DWIGHT

Jan 2-46

Happy New Year:-

Have a lot to look forward to this year - Getting out of the Army for one and it don't look like it will be too long from now until I'll be eligible to leave here.

[Envelope:]
Sgt. W.E. Musgrave 17018445
937 Ord. H.A.M. Co
A.P.O. 180 ℅ Postmaster
San Francisco Calif.

JAN 4 POSTAL SERVICE

Mr Earl Musgrave
Gordon
Nebraska

[Second page fragments:]
blocking ... rough ... 21 ... grapes ...

replaced by another and now ... going to make a guess will be in the States Feb 10 - -

As Ever your son -
Wright

January 2nd 1946

T/3 D.E. Margrave
937th Ord (HAM) Co.
A.P.O. 180 C/O Postmaster
San Francisco, Calif.

Okinawa

Happy New Year:

Have a lot to look forward to this year; getting out of the army for one. It doesn't look like it will be too long from now until I will be eligible to leave here, sometime this month. There seem to be plenty of ships here now; that is at present.

Someone raised a big stink about the way things were being handled here and the island commander was replaced by another and now the shipping seems to be pretty well in hand. My moral is pretty high now; living in hopes of leaving this place.

I am sending a few pictures that I took; they didn't come out too good. The boys that do the developing don't do too good of job and the materials they have are not the best.

I am on CQ tonight. I have to get the cooks and the K.P.s in the morning and answer the phone. It always rings during the night. Everything is about the same as always, only we don't work very hard or long hours now.

> *"There seem to be plenty of ships here now; that is at present."*

"**My moral** is ***pretty high,*** *living in hopes of leaving this place*"

The weather has been good, not much rain and it is pretty warm most of the time. It has never frosted yet, but gets a little chilly at night.

We built some oil burners for our tents. So far only two have caught on fire and we haven't burned any tents down. Pretty lucky. We use little 15 gallon drums for stoves and empty shell cases for pipes. The one in our tent works swell.

Dad, I went to a football game here yesterday, "touch football" and it is sure rough. They don't wear any padding at all. There is no tackling but the blocking and line players are just as rough as any. It was a rough game between the Marines 21 and Army 13. Some of those guys would run right over their own line backs and then hurdle the other line trying to get by without being touched. There is lots of passing in these games and both teams really had some good passers. They would just throw that ball like a bullet. They carried about a half dozen off of the field before the game was over.

I am going to make a guess that I will be in the States February 10th.

As Ever your son,
Dwight

Jan 15-45

Dear Dad:

I have got some goo[d]
news. Will be processed a[nd]
ready to leave he[re in a few]
weeks. a[nd]

...leave 17028445
M.CO.
Postmaster
...sco Calif.

JAN 17
U.S. ARMY POSTAL SERVICE

6¢ U.S. POSTAL VIA AIR MAIL

Mr. Earl Margrove
Gordon

January 15th 1946

T/3 D.E. Margrave
937th Ord (HAM) Co.
A.P.O. 180 C/O Postmaster
San Francisco, Calif.

Okinawa

Dear Dad:

I have got some good news. I will be processed and be ready to leave here this week. I am eligible for discharge now. I will probably ship out next week as there are plenty of shipping spaces available here at present. Then about 15 or 20 days at sea and I will be in the States. I will sure be glad to get out of here and out of the army.

Don't write any more as they will just come over here and back and I will probably be on my way when this letter reaches you.

I have been in about 40 months and that is really a long time. I will be discharged from Fort Logan, Colorado and then stay in Denver a few days and then on to Gordon.

This is about all for now.

I will write again before I leave and seeing you before long.

As Ever your son,
Dwight

> "I have been in about 40 months and that is really a long time. I will be discharged from Fort Logan."

DWIGHT E MARGRAVE
MILITARY SERVICE
1942 - 1946

Dwight Earl Margrave, Tech 3 Army Ordinance, Age 29, 1946.

Military Service

Dwight E. Margrave, of Gordon Nebraska, enlisted in the Army August 4th, 1942 at Fort Crook, Nebraska. He joined the 265th Ordnance Company as a Private 1st Class. He attended Automotive Maintenance School at Fort Crook, Nebraska. He was promoted to Technician 5th Grade and ultimately Technician 3rd Grade/ Technical Sergeant 3rd Grade.

Dwight was sent overseas to the Pacific War Theater in April 1945 where he served on Saipan and Okinawa. He was honorably discharged on February 15th, 1946. He was awarded the American Service Medal, Asiatic Pacific Medal, World War II Victory Medal and the Good Conduct Medal.

Irean's photo in Dwight's photo wallet for the Soldiers.

Dwight held this close to his heart during those long agonizing unspeakable days in the Pacific Theater.

State Service Office Form 53—

Certified Copy

ARMY OF THE UNITED STATES
HONORABLE DISCHARGE

This is to certify that   Dwight E. Margrave 17 078 445 Technician Third Grade
937th Ordnance Heave Automobive Maintenance   Army of the United States
is hereby Honorably Discharged from the military service of the United States of America.
This certificate is awarded as a testimonial of Honest and Faithful Service to this country.

Given at   Separation Center Fort Logan Colorado

Date: February 15, 1946.

/s/ Clemont C. Parrish
Clemont C. Parrish
Lt Colonel CAC

State of Nebraska
County of   Sheridan   } ss:

I, the undersigned, a duly commissioned Notary Public in and for the state and county aforementioned, do hereby certify that the above and foregoing together with information contained on the back hereof constitute a true, correct and accurate copy of the Discharge and Enlistment Record of the person named hereon.

Date: December 27, 1949.

Joseph F. Balday
Notary Public

(SEAL)

(OVER)

ENLISTED RECORD AND REPORT OF SEPARATION
HONORABLE DISCHARGE

1. LAST NAME FIRST NAME MIDDLE INITIAL	2. ARMY SERIAL NO.	3. GRADE	4. ARM OR SERVICE	5. COMPONENT
Margrave Dwight E	17 078 445	Tec 3	Ord	ERC

6. ORGANIZATION	7. DATE OF SEPARATION	8. PLACE OF SEPARATION
934th Ord Heavy Automotive Maint	15 Feb 46	Separation Center Ft Logan Colo

9. PERMANENT ADDRESS FOR MAILING PURPOSES	10. DATE OF BIRTH	11. PLACE OF BIRTH
Gordon Nebr	13 Jun 16	Gordon, Nebr.

12. ADDRESS FROM WHICH EMPLOYMENT WILL BE SOUGHT	13. COLOR EYES	14. COLOR HAIR	15. HEIGHT	16. WEIGHT	17. NO DEPEND
See 9	Blue	DkBr	5'11"	204 lbs.	1

18. RACE	19. MARITAL STATUS	20. U.S. CITIZEN	21. CIVILIAN OCCUPATION AND NO
WHITE X	SINGLE X	YES X	Construction Machine Operator 7-23.50

MILITARY HISTORY

22. DATE OF INDUCTION	23. DATE OF ENLISTMENT	24. DATE OF ENTRY INTO ACTIVE SERVICE	25. PLACE OF ENTRY INTO SERVICE
	4 Aug 42	14 Sep 42	Ft Crook Nebr

SELECTIVE SERVICE DATA	26. REGISTERED	27. LOCAL S.S. BOARD NO	28. COUNTY AND STATE	29. HOME ADDRESS AT TIME OF ENTRY INTO SERVICE
	YES	1	Sheridan Nebr	See 9

30. MILITARY OCCUPATIONAL SPECIALTY AND NO	31. MILITARY QUALIFICATION AND DATE
Automotive Mechanic 985	Driver & Mechanic Badge With Bar Mkm Carbine

32. BATTLES AND CAMPAIGNS
None

33. DECORATIONS AND CITATIONS
American Service Medal Asiatic Pacific Medal World War II Victory Medal Good Conduct Medal

34. WOUNDS RECEIVED IN ACTION
None

35. LATEST IMMUNIZATION DATES				36. SERVICE OUTSIDE CONTINENTAL U.S. AND RETURN		
SMALLPOX	TYPHOID	TETANUS	OTHER (specify)	DATE OF DEPARTURE	DESTINATION	DATE OF ARRIVAL
18Jan46	18Jan46	4Jan44	Cholera 20Oct45	2Dec42	American Theater	2 Dec 42
				22Mar43	US	22 Mar 43
				16Apr45	Pacific Theater	18 May 45
				Unknown	US	8Feb46

37. TOTAL LENGTH OF SERVICE						38. HIGHEST GRADE HELD
CONTINENTAL SERVICE			FOREIGN SERVICE			
YEARS	MONTHS	DAYS	YEARS	MONTHS	DAYS	Tec 3
2	3	18	1	1	14	

39. PRIOR SERVICE
None

40. REASON AND AUTHORITY FOR SEPARATION
Convenience of the Government RR1-1 (Demobilization) AR 615-365 15 Dec 44

41. SERVICE SCHOOLS ATTENDED	42. EDUCATION (Years)		
Motor School Ft Crook Nebr	Grammar	High School	College

PAY DATA

43. LONGEVITY FOR PAY PURPOSES			44. MUSTERING OUT PAY		45. SOLDIER DEPOSITS	46. TRAVEL PAY	47. TOTAL AMOUNT	NAME OF DISBURSING OFFICER
YEARS	MONTHS	DAYS	TOTAL $300	THIS PAYMENT $100	10 00	27.40	155.32	P L Rogers Maj FD
3	6	12						

INSURANCE NOTICE

IMPORTANT IF PREMIUM IS NOT PAID WHEN DUE OR WITHIN THIRTY ONE DAYS THEREAFTER, INSURANCE WILL LAPSE. MAKE CHECKS OR MONEY ORDERS PAYABLE TO THE TREASURER OF THE U. S. AND FORWARD TO COLLECTIONS SUBDIVISION, VETERANS ADMINISTRATION, WASHINGTON 25, D. C.

48. KIND OF INSURANCE			49. HOW PAID		50. Effective Date of Allotment Discontinuance	51. Date of Next Premium Due (One month after 50)	52. PREMIUM DUE EACH MONTH	53. INTENTION OF VETERAN TO		
Nat Serv	U.S. Govt.	None	Allotment	Direct to V.A.				Continue	Continue Only	Discontinue
X				X	28Feb46	31Mar46	$ 6 80			X

55. REMARKS
Lapel Button Issued ASR Score (2September1945)-44
Inactive Service ERC 4 Aug 42 to 13 Sep 42
*Typhus 26 Oct 45

56. SIGNATURE OF PERSON BEING SEPARATED	57. PERSONNEL OFFICER (Type name grade and organization signature)
/s/ Dwight E Margrave	Vesta M Arnold 1st Lt WAC /s/ Vesta M. Arnold

Army of the United States Honorable Discharge papers, February 15th 1946.

AS EVER, *Dwight*

DWIGHT E. MARGRAVE'S

After the war Dwight made a living as a **civil engineer.** He turned to his first love, construction work and was an able and **skilled** heavy equipment operator, road and dam builder. He purchased his own **International Diesel Bulldozer** in **1946** with the money he earned in the **United States Army**.

POST WAR EPILOGUE

DWIGHT EARL MARGRAVE
A SOLDIER'S JOURNEY THROUGH WWII

He will be long remembered in **Gordon, Nebraska** and nearby communities for his ability and efforts in opening roads to ranches, farms and homes during the **blizzard of 1949**, when he unselfishly made all efforts to help all those who were in need. To the community, **Dwight was a man with a cheerful disposition, empathy, and understanding for his fellow man.**

PHOTO CREDITS

PAGE XI
American fighter fly in formation over the USS MISSOURI during surrender ceremonies. Tokyo Bay, Japan. Sept. 2, 1945.
By Everett Collection

PAGE XIV
Earl Margrave, Jack Grant, Pearl Margrave, Dwight Margrave, Alta Grant, Ehel, Gene Brom, Fay Hill - 1918.
By Margrave Collection

PAGE XV
Spring Lake Ranch, Sandhills of Nebraska, USA - 1930's.
By Margrave Collection

PAGE 26
Dwight on "Pop Eye" summer of 1936 Gordon, Nebraska.
By Margrave Collection

PAGE 80
Pearl Harbor: Battered by bombs and torpedoes, U.S.S. California Evacuated as sailors and soldiers look on, December 7, 1941.
By Everett Collection

PAGE 82
World War II, Pearl Harbor, Hawaii, the destruction of the USS West Virginia, December 7, 1941, official U.S. Navy photograph.
By Everett Collection

PAGE 83
The wreckage of the destroyers USS Downes and USS Cassin at Pearl Harbor dry dock.
By Everett Collection

PAGE 116
"Miss Never Sail", image is in the public domain in the United States.

PAGE 142
A post-war model of 'Little Boy' the atomic bomb exploded over Hiroshima, Japan, in World War II.
By Everett Collection

PAGE 157
Aerial view, K25 Plant, Oak Ridge site of the Manhattan Project. 1947 (photo by Ed Westcott).
By Everett Collection

PAGE 250
Battleship USS Pennsylvania is followed by cruisers. January 1945. Philippines, Pacific Ocean, World War II.

PAGE 274
Enola Gay' landing after the atomic bombing mission on Hiroshima, Japan. Tinian, Marianas Islands. August 6, 1945.
By Everett Collection

PHOTO CREDITS

PAGE 288
'Trinity' explosion at Los Alamos, Alamogordo, New Mexico. July 16, 1945. Manhattan Project, World War II.
By Everett Collection

PAGE 292
The battleship USS Idaho shelling Okinawa on April 1st, 1945.
National Photo Archives

PAGE 294
Atomic bomb. Hiroshima, Japan after the atomic bomb was dropped by the US bomber "Enola Gay" 1945.
By Everett Collectio

PAGE 298
August 9th, 1945, another atomic bomb was dropped on the Japanese city Nagasaki,
By Everett Collectio

PAGE 314
Landing craft of supply U.S. forces on Okinawa. April 13, 1945.
By Everett Collection

PAGE 304
The super battleship Yamato explodes after persistent attacks from US aircraft, April 7th 1945.
By National Photo Archives

PAGE 320
Soldiers clearing Okinawa with Thompson submachine guns after heavy shelling by the U.S. Navy.
By National Photo Archives

PAGE 324
Personnel surveying the debris and the severely damaged USS Ocelot (IX-110) and USS Nestor (ARB-6) caused by Typhoon Louise at Buckner Bay, Okinawa, in October 1945.
By US Navy Photo

PAGE 356
Earl Margrave after the War on his tractor, Gordon, Nebraska.
By Margrave Collecton

Made in United States
Orlando, FL
26 August 2022